D0532739

Our world
Displays

VICTORIA FARROW

AUTHOR VICTORIA FARROW

EDITOR JANE BISHOP

ASSISTANT EDITORS LESLEY SUDLOW AND SALLY GRAY

SERIES DESIGNER LYNNE JOESBURY

DESIGNER RACHEL WARNER

ILLUSTRATIONS GAYNOR BERRY

With thanks to my class of nursery children at Polwhele House School, Truro, Cornwall who helped to produce the displays in this book.
To my family, Richard, Ben and Rachel and the staff of the Pre-prepatory department for their support and encouragement.

Designed using Adobe Pagemaker

Published by Scholastic Ltd, Villiers House, Clarendon Avenue, Leamington Spa, Warwickshire CV32 5PR
Text © Victoria Farrow

© 2000 Scholastic Ltd

1 2 3 4 5 6 7 8 9 0   0 1 2 3 4 5 6 7 8 9

British Library Cataloguing-in-Publication Data
A catalogue record for this book is available from the British Library.

ISBN 0-439-01738-6

Contents

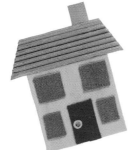

Introduction

Aims of successful displays

A child's world is full of change, challenges and exciting things to learn about. Being able to keep up to date with the interests of the children in your care is a challenge in itself. The added pressure of creating a visually stimulating environment with displays to match each new project can seem daunting.

The main aim of this book is to provide stimulating ideas for exciting, interactive displays that will brighten the children's environment and form an important part of their learning experiences. They are intended to be used by all early years practitioners, and do not require any specialist knowledge or equipment.

The themes covered in this book are based on various aspects of the children's worlds: their homes and those of animals and fictional characters, journeys they take in reality or in their imagination, places they visit, people who help them, and the constantly changing weather.

Each theme is supported by ideas for five wall displays, a stimulus display to get the project underway and a table-top display for the children to use. The displays are intended to be as interactive as possible, to promote learning through play and to bring the displays to life.

All of the displays have been tried and tested in a working nursery. Learning objectives for the displays aim to meet the requirements of the Early Learning Goals identified by the Qualifications and Curriculum Authority.

Photocopiable sheets at the end of the book provide templates to use for displays and borders.

Ideas are provided to make displays that can:
- cover awkward areas of the room
- be removed at the end of the session
- provide a central focus to a theme
- promote Early Learning Goals
- encompass a variety of creative skills.

A display can be effectively used to:
- provide a cheerful and stimulating environment
- give confidence to parents and guardians regarding the standard of care and commitment provided
- provide a record of work undertaken
- promote discussion
- give children pride in their work and develop their self-confidence
- aid learning.

Planning

Before you start a new theme, it is best to plan which of the displays you are going to make and where you will be able to position them. Plan the order in which you intend to make the displays and make sure that interactive displays have a table-top or work surface that can be placed in front of the display board, even if it is on a temporary basis. Make use of the area outside the main door, where parents often gather, for an

Introduction

eye-catching board display. Pin up newsletters telling parents about the themes that their children will be working on and asking for any contributions for objects for display tables that can be loaned from home. Make requests for extra adult help at certain sessions where assistance is needed, for example when the children are going to the park, or to help with papier mâché in the classroom.

The 'Home links' ideas provided for the displays could also be pinned on a board outside the door. These give suggestions for activities that parents may wish to do with their children to extend and reinforce the work done in the group.

Difficult displays

Unsightly or awkward wall space can be disguised with corrugated paper that comes in rolls of different colours. The paper will stand up and undulate to curve around pipes or other fittings. It can also be used to make a temporary display where a display board is not available. By attaching the paper to a heavy tin or brick, positioned behind and out of sight, the paper will be kept anchored and upright. By cutting the top edge in an undulating wave shape as in the table-top display for 'Blow wind blow', page 36, the paper takes on a softer feel which is more pleasing on the eye.

'At the airport' table-top display, page 72, uses a backdrop of card that leans against the wall. This display can be temporary and could cover another display that will remain unharmed behind it. This is particularly useful if you share your room with a number of other groups.

Making use of toys and play situations

Where possible, the stimulus displays use toys and materials found in most early years groups. The stimulus display for 'Homes', page 49, uses a table-top with diggers, sand, bricks and play people. These in themselves will act as a magnet, drawing children to come and play! The activity can easily be extended into the sand tray where children can build homes in the sand and have fun experimenting with wet and dry sand. Similarly, the water tray can be used to float the sailing boats made for the 'Blow wind blow' display, page 36, along with other ideas suggested in 'What to do' on that page.

A road-mat is used for small-world play in the chapter on 'People who help us', and the children can use play people to act out the role of the crossing patrol person in 'Crossing the road', page 20, or the role of the postman in 'Delivering the mail', page 14, while indirectly learning about direction, positional language and road safety.

Resources

Make use of the local library for a constantly renewable source of books to add to displays and encourage children to read and develop a love of books. It is worth buying those books, however, that will be used over and over again.

A collection of laminated pictures cut out from copies of *Child Education*, *Infant Projects* or *Nursery Projects* (Scholastic) is very useful for display purposes. Laminating keeps the pictures clean and allows children to handle them without spoiling them. 'Rainbows' display, page 30, uses a set of colour pictures taken from *Nursery Projects* 'Colours', issue no 1. These could also be used for colour sorting or individual colour tables. By simply covering a table with red fabric, placing a red hoop in the centre and asking the children to find 'red' items to place inside the hoop, you have an instant red display.

Pictures cut from magazines, catalogues, holiday brochures and calendars can be stored and kept for future projects.

Pieces of fabric large enough to cover a table or hang as a backdrop are a very useful, versatile and attractive resource. The stimulus display for 'Journeys', page 61, uses a piece of deep blue fabric to display a simple array of toy vehicles. Fabric is used to extend the length of 'The woods' display, page 42, so that leaves, twigs, bark, clay toadstools and books can be arranged at the base of the display by pinning fabric over a shelving unit.

Introduction

Materials and techniques

Displays always look more effective if you take time to choose bright, eye-catching colours. If the paper available appears too dull, try sponge painting it with powder paint to make a more interesting backing paper. The sky in 'The three little pigs' display, page 50 (and opposite), uses this technique to add colour and texture. In 'A ride on a steam train', page 70, several painting techniques are combined to make an exciting display using plain sugar paper and powder paints. In 'A view from the window', page 58, a special display was made using children's individual paintings that were framed with card window frames and decorated with window boxes made from odds and ends found in the collage box.

A border around a display makes a special finishing touch. Cut strips of paper and print with a repeating pattern or cut out and stick shapes from bright coloured paper. Alternatively, use rolls of 'border roll' in contrasting colours. These are available in a wide range of colours in plain and corrugated paper, cut straight or with an undulating edge. They can be pinned around the edge of the display and reused several times.

Putting up the display

Having backed the display board, use Blu-Tack or drawing pins to hold individual pieces of the display in place until you are satisfied with the arrangement. Use the staple gun sparingly as removing the staples afterwards is difficult and the children's work can become torn and spoiled.

Take time to make sure that lettering and labels are eye-catching and neat. Writing or cutting out letters for the heading can often seem time-consuming, but it can make all the difference to the end result.

Making displays interactive

A display that is at child height with a work surface or table in front of it can really draw the children's attention and natural curiosity. Children love to touch items on display, so it is so much more positive to actively encourage them to touch the display than to constantly remind them not to. As well as providing items that the children have

brought in or made in the group, provide table displays where the children are encouraged to play with the items on display, or a counting or science-based display where the children are asked to find things out, to experiment or to build.

'The three little pigs' display, page 50, asks the children to compare all the materials on display and use them to build houses with. Show the children the display as a group and encourage them to compare the texture, weight and strength of their materials. Ask them which of the materials are best for building with and why.

Teaching the children how to use the display enables them to get as much from the learning opportunity as possible and helps them to find out things for themselves. Children will naturally play with the materials and can gain a great deal from a suitably set up display table with little adult intervention.

Providing play people, toy animals or puppets allows the children to act out a story or rhyme illustrated in a display. In 'The duck pond', page 44, the children

are provided with plastic ducks for counting on and off a pond, paper plate puppets to use while singing the rhyme and a glove puppet to play with and talk to while reading *Daisy Duck* or *Five Little Ducks*. This display is packed with interactive props that can lead to a wide variety of imaginative play as well as excellent hands-on mathematical experiences.

'The firefighter' display, page 16, allows the children free expression with small-world toys, letting them act out a rescue using toy fire-engines, play people and buildings made by themselves. By using adult intervention, the children can learn valuable mathematical lessons by being asked which number house the firefighters have been called to, whether the ladder is long enough to reach the top window and so on.

A basket of leaves, twigs and bark in 'The woods' display, page 42, provides a stimulating introduction to textures and touch as well as providing a starting point for extended vocabulary as the children try to come up with words to describe what they can see and touch.

Displays that are well set up provide a wealth of valuable learning situations for children to use with little adult help. Encouraging the children to take care of the displays and tidy them when they have finished playing with them is good practice and prolongs the life of the displays, as well as encouraging the children to have pride in their work.

Providing books with displays that the children can share and return is a great incentive towards independent reading and a love of books. Look out for suitable books to go with the displays and try to provide both fiction and non-fiction titles.

Stimulus

A stimulus display is used to introduce each new theme. It should be simple and easy to put together, and just as easy to put away again. The display can be set up at the beginning of the session before the children arrive to draw their attention as they enter the room – something new, exciting and stimulating.

Set up these displays at child height so that they can gather round and look as the new theme is introduced. The stimulus display for 'People who help us', page 13, uses boxes covered in coloured paper on which display items, pictures and books are arranged. The display takes only minutes to put together but states clearly what the theme is and shows what the children will be learning about. It looks impressive, showing planning and organization.

The weather chart used as a stimulus for 'Weather', page 25, takes longer to make but is an excellent permanent resource that can be used every day.

Table-top displays

Brightly-coloured card can be folded to provide a backdrop for a display of models on a fabric-covered table. By using models made by the children, or a collection of items brought together by the children in the group, a simple yet eye-catching display can be made with the minimum of effort.

Decorative stars or other items can be attached to the card to make it more interesting or the shape of the card can be altered by cutting the top edge to

Introduction

make waves or zigzags. The card used in the backdrop for 'Made from wood', page 48, is cut to suggest the shape of treetops and makes a far more interesting shape than an ordinary flat edge would have.

Hang fabric, a wallcovering or create another display to cover pipes or other unsightly objects. Cover a table or worktop with a cloth or piece of bright fabric and then, by putting bricks or boxes under the fabric, create an interesting surface on which items can be displayed at different heights.

Make a display case by sticking boxes together and covering them with coloured paper. Tins and other containers can be covered with coloured paper and used to display items like the windmills in 'Blow wind blow', page 36. Whole boxes can be covered with paper and used to stick artwork onto to make a kind of display totem pole. Items can also be put on top of the boxes. These displays would be easy to dismantle.

Photographs and other images

Parents love to see photographs of their children on display. By selecting photos of the children at work you can create a simple, effective display that everyone can enjoy. Get into the habit of taking pictures of the children involved in everyday activities as well as the more special events.

Photographs provide instant records of events that are particularly useful for record-keeping as well as display work. In the stimulus display 'Places', page 37, photographs of children and places visited are used to form the basis of the display and stimulate the children's interest. Children love to see photographs of themselves and places they know and the photographs help them to recall places and events or people who have left the group. They can be used to help with sequencing of events and to show how the children have grown and changed.

Computer programs include a wide selection of clip art that can be used to decorate stimulus displays or provide decorative borders to lettering. The stimulus display for 'Places', page 37, uses clip art pictures which are cut out and interspersed among the photographs, while the individual

headings make use of decorative borders to give them a special touch. This display also uses stencil paper to make simple pictures that are cut out and printed with poster or powder paint. The stencils were later used by the children who had great fun producing exciting pictures with images that they would not have been able to paint freehand.

Lettering

Quality lettering gives displays a professional look and provides an example to the children, encouraging them to read the words or identify the letters that they have learned. Use lettering on display tables to label individual items, as in the table-top display for 'Made from wood', page 48. Here the individual letters for the word 'Wood' are cut out of brown card, while the labels for the display items are printed using a word processor in much smaller letters. However, providing too many labels can be overwhelming.

Either make use of a computer to print out headings or alternatively draw around wooden or plastic letter templates to make sure that your display has clear, attractive lettering. It is worth laminating labels if the display is to be left out for a while and handled by the children. The laminated words can be kept in a word bank and reused.

Parental involvement

Displays are an excellent way of showing parents and visiting adults what is going on in the group. They provide examples of the quality of work produced in the group and discussion points between adults and children.

To involve parents in the display process, pin up newsletters explaining what you are doing and asking for items such as egg boxes, newspapers or other odds and ends. In the chapter, 'People who help us', page 13, it is suggested that a recycling point is chosen to encourage parents to bring in old newspapers or junk materials to be used for

modelling (see page 18). This helps parents to become actively involved and provides children with a link between home and the group. The ideas provided at the end of each display entitled 'Home links' suggests activities for parents to do at home with their children to extend the work done in each theme.

Curriculum opportunities

Each of the displays covered in the book provides opportunities for the six areas of learning covered in the Early Learning Goals to be explored. Ideas are provided for each area, so that making the display becomes the focus of the theme. Decide on which displays to try before you start a new theme to achieve a far more rounded and well-planned project.

Making displays provides endless opportunities for children to learn social skills as they get used to taking turns, sharing out materials, working together and helping to clear up. There are valuable lessons to be learned in mathematics and science as the children mix colours and find out about the different shades and blends. The names of shapes can be learned as they print repeating patterns and use shaped paper in many different forms.

2-D and 3-D displays

Three-dimensional displays always look special and it is worth always having one special display that stands out.

snails

THEMES ON DISPLAY
for early years

Remember that it is easier to suspend items from the ceiling or stand them on a display table rather than try to attach heavy items to display boards.

Hoops covered with crêpe paper make good bases for mobiles hung from the ceiling or beams such as the rain and sun mobiles in the 'Rainbows' display, page 30. A branch stuck in a bucket of sand makes a wonderful tree that can be hung with birds, flowers and so on. Ribbon or twisted crêpe paper can be pinned to the display board and stretched over a table in front of the board. This gives a good 3-D effect for ideas such as showing the rays of the sun. The canopy in 'The market place' display, page 38, is slightly more complicated but provides a stunning display and is well worth the extra effort involved.

'The gingerbread house', page 54, is made from a large cardboard box and as well as being great fun to make, forms a mobile display that can be moved from place to place. Similarly, 'The rubbish monster', page 18, is made from a collection of junk material, and as well as being inexpensive to make, helps teach the children about the importance of recycling materials.

Giving an otherwise two-dimensional display, a degree of the third-dimension can be simply done by curving card items, such as the fir trees at the bottom of the 'The woods' display, page 42, so that they stand out from the wall. Attach the edges of the card to the board with Blu-Tack or staple them securely in place.

People who help us

Helping each other

Learning objectives: to become familiar with the different people who help us; to ask questions about who they are and what they do.

What you need
A collection of heavy-duty cardboard boxes in a variety of sizes; sheets of brightly-coloured craft paper in two or three colours; sticky tape; Blu-Tack or sticky Velcro; pictures of fire-engines, police-officers, children in hospital and so on; play people and vehicles for the 'People who help us' theme; non-fiction books such as the *People Who Help Us* series (Wayland) or story-books about *Postman Pat* by John Cunliffe (Hippo) and *Fireman Sam* by Rob Lee (Heinemann).

What to do
Choose a box that will cover approximately half of your display table and cover it with brightly-coloured craft paper. Cover and arrange two or three smaller boxes on top to make an attractive arrangement. Select a few brightly-coloured pictures of 'People who help us' and laminate them if possible. Attach them to the sides of the boxes using sticky Velcro pads or Blu-Tack. Add play people, toy vehicles and books. Make a sign saying 'People who help us' by hand writing on a piece of folded card and place it in front of or on top of one of the boxes.

Invite the children to come and sit in a group around you where they can all see the display and be drawn into conversation.

Talk about
● Using the 'Can I help you?' photocopiable sheet on page 73, see if the children can identify and name the different people shown.
● Talk about the people who work for the emergency services, their role in the community and the fact that they wear special uniforms to make them instantly recognizable and to protect them.
● Encourage the children to think of ways that they can help each other, such as helping younger children put on coats and offering friendship.
● Introduce 999 as the emergency services number. Stress that it should only be used to call in a real emergency.

Home links
● Invite parents or friends who work for the emergency services to come in and talk to the children about their work.
● Invite a worker from your group, such as a premises officer, to talk to the children about the job that they do.

The colourful displays in this chapter will help children to find about some of the people who help us, including firefighters, hospital workers and refuse collectors.

Delivering the mail

Learning objectives: to develop a basic understanding of a route and what maps are for; to observe and identify features in the immediate environment.

What you need

Three large pieces of green card; a pencil; green, brown, red and pink tissue paper; scraps of wool; gummed paper; black paper; brown backing paper; a large piece of coloured card; pens; glue; Blu-Tack; a toy post van and post-box; letters and stamps; a selection of parcels; scales; maps; a postperson's hat and bag; books such as *Postman Pat* by John Cunliffe (Hippo) and *Teddy Bear Postman* by Phoebe and Selby Worthington (Viking Kestrel).

What to do

Take three pieces of green card and tape them together. Place the card onto a work surface, mark out an imaginary route and draw in the road with a pen. Divide up the countryside into fields and gardens, drawing the outlines with a pencil. Choose collage materials to cover the fields with and help the children to glue them into place. Use as many different shades of green for the fields and grass as you can and different materials for the crops.

Give the children green paper to tear up and stick onto small tree shapes to make leaves. Add scrunched coloured tissue paper to make apples or blossom. Give the children rectangles of paper to use as houses and ask them to stick on triangles of gummed paper for the roof and to draw on the windows and doors using a pen.

Make a post van using card covered with red gummed paper, adding black paper wheels. Attach the van to the road using Blu-Tack. Pin up the completed backdrop on the wall. Write out a heading for the display on a large piece of coloured card and position it above the wall display.

Place any available items on a table in front of the display. These could include a toy post van and post-box, letters and stamps, parcels to be sorted according to size or weight, scales, maps, a postperson's hat and bag and any available books.

Talk about

● Think about the journey of a letter from the post-box to your door. Explain how the letters are sorted and sent by mail train, post van or even airmail

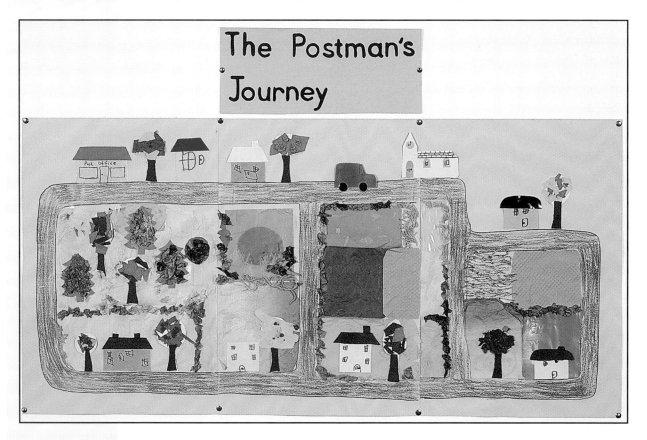

before being delivered to the door by the local postal worker.

● As the children watch, sketch out a simple map on a large piece of paper starting with a road. Draw squares for houses and use green crayon for fields. Draw a simple key at the bottom and show the children how to read it. Let the children draw maps of their own.

● Encourage the children to think about their journey to the group. Ask them to describe which route they take, 'we go past the garage and cross the main road by the school'. Encourage them to use the correct positional terms (next to, beside, across) as they talk.

Home links

● Ask the children to look out for the postperson at home and note what time the post arrives.

● Help each child to make a simple map of their journey to the group.

Using the display

Personal, social and emotional development

● Make cards to send to friends.

● Read *Katie Morag Delivers the Mail* by Mairi Hedderwick (Red Fox) where Katie muddles up the mail. Discuss helping each other and asking others for help.

Language and literacy

● Use the display for story-telling and language development, moving the post van along the road as the story proceeds.

● Ask the children to describe the route that the post van took and where they think it will go next.

● Set up a post office with an 'open' and 'closed' sign and a sorting office with pigeon holes for each child where they can send messages and pictures to each other. Write notes to the children or send them stickers for achievement.

Mathematical development

● Develop an understanding of direction by using the words 'forwards', 'backwards', 'turn', 'near', 'far'. Use a road-mat with cars and ask the children to follow specific instructions to check their understanding of directional terms.

● Help the children to judge distances by estimating which would be the quickest route to a given destination.

Knowledge and understanding of the world

● Take photos of features in your local environment. Go for a walk together and see if the children can find the real objects to match the photos.

● Make a table-top landscape with a road-mat. Add trees, buildings and cars. Which route would you take to get from A to B?

Physical development

● Read *I'm Going on a Bear Hunt* by Michael Rosen (Walker) then set up an obstacle course with hoops to represent pools of mud, ropes to mark out the river and so on. Act out the story as a group.

The firefighter

Learning objectives: to show that firefighters help to put out fires; to ask questions about how things happen and why.

What you need

Dark blue backing paper; red and black craft paper; gold card; powder paints; mixing plates; rectangular printing sponges; black and off-white sugar paper; red, yellow and white tissue paper; PVA glue; toy fire-engines; play people; books such as *Fireman Sam* by Rob Lee (Heinemann), *Fire Engines* in the *Mighty Machines* series, by Caroline Bingham (Dorling Kindersley) and *Firefighter* in the *People Who Help Us* series (Wayland); cereal boxes; coloured craft paper.

What to do

Cover the display board with dark blue backing paper and add the heading '999' cut from gold card. Make large rectangular buildings from black sugar paper with the windows cut out.

Explain that you are going to make a display of a fire-engine with the firefighters putting out a fire. Ask the children to suggest what colours you might need for your picture then give a group of children a box of tissue paper and ask them to select flame colours. Discuss the colours that they have chosen and invite them to tear the tissue into strips. Provide another group of children with plates of grey paint and rectangular sponges and help them to print brick shapes onto the black paper buildings. Attach the buildings to the display board and stick tissue flames coming out of the 'windows' with white tissue for smoke.

Show the children one of the *Fireman Sam* story-books or look at a toy fire-engine. Ask them what the number is on top of the display board and why it is there. Ask the children to help you by painting firefighters to come and put out the fire. Give each child in the group a piece of sugar paper of the size you require for the finished people. As the children watch, paint a firefighter yourself, discussing the uniform and colours as you paint. Now ask the children to make their own paintings of firefighters. Remind them to fill the paper and include boots, helmets and buttons. Cut out a bright red fire-engine and add it to the picture.

Additional items can include a person positioned in a window of a building calling for help and a ladder for the firefighters to carry. Add a toy fire-engine, ladder and hose, *Fireman Sam* story-books and factual books about firefighters, houses made from cardboard boxes covered with craft paper and painted with windows and doors for the toy ladder to reach and finally some play people to climb the ladder and drive the fire-engine.

Talk about
● Think about other ways that firefighters help us, such as helping at road accidents, rescuing people and animals, dealing with chemical spills and clearing up after floods and storms.
● Discuss ways to keep safe, such as never touching matches and keeping away from hot saucepans.
● Talk about why firefighters wear bright colours and how they protect themselves from the flames and smoke.

Home links
● Ask parents to discuss safety in the home with their children. Do they have a smoke alarm or fire extinguisher at home?
● Ask some of the parents to join you on a trip to the local fire station with the children.

Using the display
Personal, social and emotional development
● Discuss ways of helping each other: putting on coats; passing round the crayons; remembering to show new children where things are kept.
● Ask, 'Who do we ask when we need help?'. Think of different situations and ask, 'Who would help you?'.

Mathematical development
● Use play figures to develop positional language, talking to the children as they play. Ask, 'Is the ladder long enough to reach the window?'.
● Firefighters have to act quickly and fire-engines are driven fast. Sort pictures of cars, rockets, snails and tortoises into sets of 'fast' and 'slow'.

Knowledge and understanding of the world
● Have a practice fire drill at your group and discuss what to do in case of fire.
● Role-play using the telephone. Discuss how and when it should be used, emphasizing that the telephone number 999 is for emergencies only.

Physical development
● Draw a chalk ladder on the ground with the numbers up to ten; one on each rung. Ask the children to jump on each rung in turn and say the number. Can they come back down again? Rub out a number and ask them to jump over the missing number. Which number is missing?
● Climb ladders and slide down poles in a game of firefighters.
● Run fast and walk very slowly. Try out other speeds as you move around the room.

People who
help us

THEMES ON DISPLAY
for early years

A rubbish monster

Learning objectives: to develop care for the environment; to talk about features that are liked and disliked.

What you need
Plastic bin liner; a large card cylinder; blue and purple tissue paper; a circle of card to match the opening of the cylinder; PVA glue; two cardboard cones; silver paint; white corrugated paper; two pulp paper balls; marker pen; scissors; green card; newspaper; glitter glue; *Recycle Rubbish* in the *I Can Help* series (Franklin Watts).

What to do
Collect some of the 'junk' items on the list above, making sure that they are all clean and safe. Place them in a bin liner and sit in front of your group. Ask the children what they think is in your bag.

Explain that you forgot to put your bin out for the refuse collectors and thought you might leave it somewhere else. Do they think tipping it out in the park or school playground would be a good idea? Where do they think your rubbish should go? Do they always put their sweet wrappers and empty cans in the bin?

Tip your bag of clean rubbish onto the floor in front of the children and see how they react. Does anyone have a better idea for these items rather than putting them in the bin? Have they heard of recycling? What does it mean? Share the book *Recycle Rubbish* with the group.

Explain that you are going to make a rubbish-eating monster out of some of the rubbish from your bag. Start by taping the card circle to the back of the card cylinder then add horns to the top made from cardboard cones. Ask the children to help tear newspaper into strips and glue it all over the card model to add substance to the monster. Finish with a couple of layers of purple and blue tissue paper and paint a layer of PVA glue to act as a varnish. Cut out green card arms and legs for the monster and paint on toe-nails with

glitter glue. Paint the horns with silver paint. Attach two pulp balls to the head for eyes, adding black centres with a marker pen. The teeth are cut from lengths of white corrugated paper in a zigzag fashion and taped to the inside of the mouth. The rubbish monster is now ready to gobble up rubbish!

Use the display to promote recycling and putting rubbish in the bin. Encourage the children to think about what different materials items are made of. Label the display 'I eat rubbish', or make a sign which can be changed such as 'Our monster eats paper today'.

Talk about
● Ask the children if they can remember what materials were used to make the monster and where the materials came from.
● Discuss the reasons for saving and recycling paper. Do the children think a paper bank would be a good idea?
● Talk about the area that the children live in, the features they like and dislike.

Home links
● Make a collection point where boxes and useful items can be brought in from home and used for 'junk modelling'.
● Tell the children to watch out for the refuse collectors at home and to find out which day they come to empty the bins.

Using the display
Personal, social and emotional development
● Remind the children to wash their hands after they have been cleaning or picking up rubbish. When else should you wash your hands?
● Spring-clean your room and encourage the children to have pride in their own space.
● Discuss caring for the environment and keeping it safe for people and animals.
● Set aside a recycling box at your group for waste paper.

Language and literacy
● Design posters to encourage people to reuse and recycle.
● Use old newspapers and magazines to cut out letters and words.

Mathematical development
● Play 'Ten green bottles'. Line up ten plastic bottles weighted with sand and knock them over with beanbags. How many have you knocked over? How many are left?
● Sort items according to the materials that they are made of – plastic, paper, metal or wood.

Physical development
● Play at collecting rubbish – throw balls into bins or beanbags into hoops.
● See how many bricks the children can load into a toy truck; imagine that they are boxes of newspaper to be recycled.

Creative development
● Make a display of junk models made from materials brought in from home.
● Print patterns using scrunched-up newspaper or rags dipped in paint.
● Make collages using just one type of material – paper, plastic, metal or wood.

Crossing the road

Learning objectives: to learn about road safety; to consider the consequences of actions on self and others.

What you need
Backing paper; powder paints; sugar paper; coloured activity paper; copies of *The Green Cross Code* (HMSO); books such as *Mrs Jollipop* by Dick King-Smith (Macdonald Young) or *Look Out on the Road* from RoSPA (The Safety Education Dept, RoSPA, Edgbaston Park, 353 Bristol Road, Birmingham B5 7ST).

What to do
Show the children a picture of a crossing patrol person or a plastic play figure dressed accordingly. Ask the children if they know who this person is and what they do to help us. If the children see a crossing patrol person working nearby refer to this.

Explain that you are going to make a display showing how the crossing patrol person helps us to cross the road safely. Ask the children to paint pictures of themselves and hand out pieces of paper cut to the desired size. Encourage the children to look carefully at each other before they start, to see where the facial features are, where the arms come from and so on. When complete, leave the paintings to dry.

Cover the display board with blue paper and add some simple buildings to the background cut from brown or grey sugar paper. Add a grey paper road to the front of the picture. If you wish, add a zebra crossing made from black and white paper or paint.

Ask one of the children to help you paint the crossing patrol person, making sure that the figure is quite a bit taller than the pictures of the children. Add a uniform and a lollipop stick to hold.

Sketch out the shape of a car and ask another child to paint it for you. When all the paintings are dry, cut them out and add them to the display. Position the 'children' so that they are lined up waiting to cross the road. Position the car so that it has stopped at the sign of the lollipop. To finish off the display, cut out lots of paper circles and write the word 'Stop' on each one. Arrange them at regular intervals around the edge of the display.

Place a copy of *The Green Cross Code*, stories and non-fiction books, a crossing patrol play person, play people and cars on the display table.

Talk about
● Discuss safe places to cross the road – with a crossing patrol person, at a zebra or pelican crossing.
● Emphasize that children should always cross the road with an adult.

Home links
● Talk through *The Green Cross Code* with the children and give them a copy to take home to share with their family.

● Ask a group of parents to help you take the children out and show them how to cross over the road safely with an adult.

Using the display
Language and literacy
● Ask the question, 'Why do we need to listen as well as look when we are waiting to cross the road?'. Encourage the children in their responses.
● Play some listening games such as sound lotto to improve the children's listening skills.
● Learn to recognize the word 'stop' by playing word lotto or snap.

Mathematical development
● Make a road-safety game with play people and toy cars. Line the people up at the side of the road and walk the crossing patrol person into the centre of the road. Make the cars stop. Let the children take turns at throwing the dice and moving that number of people across the road, one at a time.
● Make a game using a selection of different-coloured and different-sized cards. Draw symbols on them and ask the children to take one and match it to an object. For example a small red bear or a large green bear.

Knowledge and understanding of the world
● To find out about speed and impact, throw a ball at a wall or push a toy car at a cardboard box. Point out to the children that the faster things move, the more difficult it is for them to stop.
● Compare bright colours and camouflage with the children Ask, 'When do we want to be seen and when do we want to keep hidden?'.

Physical development
● Use skipping ropes to mark out a road on the ground and in role-play let the children explore the best way to cross a road safely.
● Play a game of traffic lights with green for go and red for stop.
● Use the road-mat to reinforce the ideas of cars stopping to let children cross the road.
● Make a lollipop stick out of a length of broom handle and a card circle with 'stop' written on it. Play traffic games and let the children take turns at being the crossing patrol person.

A visit to the hospital

Learning objectives: to develop positive ideas about going into hospital; to be responsive to significant experiences, showing a range of feelings.

What you need
Newspaper; powder paints; sugar paper; sponge rollers; printing shapes; craft paper; collage scraps; yellow backing paper; scissors; Art Straws; a toy medical kit; dolls; teddy bears; a play phone; notepad and paper; books such as *Nurse* and *In Hospital* in the *People Who Help Us* series (Wayland) and *Hospital* in the *Busy Places* series by Carole Watson (Watts).

What to do
Set up the home corner as a hospital with a cushion and a blanket for a bed, a teddy bear and a picture book. Ask the children if they have ever been into hospital as a patient or if they have visited anyone in hospital.

Taking the part of the doctor or nurse show the children what is in the doctor's kit and what each piece of equipment is for. Ask one of the children to play the part of the patient or use a doll or teddy bear. Ask the patient appropriate questions and suggest how they might be treated. Let the children take turns at being the patient, the receptionist and the doctor until they are confident about taking on the roles without adult help.

Explain that you are going to make a display about going into hospital and you need some help to print bright, colourful material to use as the hospital curtains and bed cover.

Cover a painting table with newspaper and put out enough plates of paint, sponges and paper for a group of six to eight children. Give the children sponge rollers and show them how to dip them into the paint so that the rollers are well covered. Let them practise with the rollers making stripes up and down the page. When the children have made some even stripes, ask them to choose a contrasting colour

and dip shaped sponges into the paint and print on top of the stripes at regular intervals. A third colour can be added. Choose two of the patterns to use in your display.

Cover the display board in yellow paper and use some of the roller printed paper to make a 'curtain' down the right-hand side. Draw two bed heads to the required size, paint them black and cut them out. Using a second piece of printed paper for the bed cover, assemble the bed using white paper for the pillow.

Ask a group of children to paint the characters for the display, making sure that you give them guidelines as to the size, sketching the outlines if necessary.

To finish off the picture, add a table with flowers made from collage scraps and Art Straw stems. Add a toy medical kit and books about going into hospital, a bandaged teddy and a doctor's or nurse's outfit to the display table.

Talk about
● Encourage the children to share their experiences of going to the doctor or visiting the hospital. Promote positive attitudes by explaining that the doctors are kind and are there to help.
● Discuss ways of caring such as taking other children to an adult if they feel unwell and being kind to them.
● Think of ways to help cheer up people who are ill or unhappy, such as making 'get well' cards for a child from the group who is away sick.

Home links
● If you have a nurse or doctor among the parents, invite them to come in and talk to the children.

Using the display
Language and literacy
● Use role-play to encourage the children to explain why they have come to see the doctor. Help them to describe where the pain is and what it feels like.
● Use a toy telephone to call the surgery and make an appointment.
● Discuss what you would pack to take to hospital. Pack some items into a bag and see if the children can remember what is inside.
● Together, say the rhyme 'Miss Polly Had a Dolly' in *This Little Puffin...* compiled by Elizabeth Matterson (Puffin).

Mathematical development
● Make repeating patterns. Collect wallpaper samples to compare and then ask the children to print repeating patterns of their own.
● Thread beads or cotton reels using two or three colours to make repeating patterns. Draw patterns onto strips of card for the children to copy, then ask them to continue the pattern.

Knowledge and understanding of the world
● Use play figures to explain the role of the doctor, nurse and ambulance driver.
● Explain the dangers of eating or drinking unknown substances.

Creative development
● Make beds for teddies and dolls out of shoeboxes and scraps of material.
● Make some paper flowers to take to the dolls in hospital.

Table-top display

THEMES ON DISPLAY for early years

Posting games

Learning objectives: to learn to sort objects into sets; to work as part of a group, taking turns and sharing fairly.

What you need
Three good quality shoeboxes (plain white if possible); poster paints; coloured card; sticky Velcro squares; newspaper; paintbrushes; pens.

What to do
Cut a posting hole in the front of each of the three shoeboxes. Cover the floor with newspaper and paint the boxes with three layers of poster colour. Taking a contrasting colour paint, dip the brush into the pot and flick the paint over the box to give a splattered effect. Leave the boxes to dry.

The posting boxes can be used to sort shapes, colours, letters, numbers or words. Cut out and laminate sets of cards, attach a sticky Velcro square to one of each type that can then be attached to the top of the boxes. Divide the cards among two or three children or leave them in a central pile. The children can post the cards into the box with the matching picture on its lid. This is a self-correcting game where the children can remove the lids from the boxes at the end of the game and check to see if the correct cards were posted into the box.

Talk about
● How does the postperson know which houses to post the letters in? Why we put stamps on our letters?
● What happens to letters and parcels that are too big to fit in the letter box?

Home links
● Ask parents to help their children to learn their home addresses.
● Suggest that parents encourage their children to look at the numbers on the doors as they walk along the road.

Further display table ideas
● Make a row of houses out of cereal boxes covered in coloured paper. Number the houses from 1 to 10. Fill a box with envelopes or postcards, each with a number on from one to ten. Let the children take turns at posting the letters to the houses by matching the numbers.

OUR WORLD

Weather

A weather chart

Learning objectives: to recognize and name different weather types; to look closely at similarities, differences, patterns and change in weather.

What you need
A piece of A1 stiff board; brightly-coloured craft paper; sticky Velcro pads; white and brightly-coloured card; a marker pen; the photocopiable sheet on page 74 copied onto brightly-coloured paper; books such as *Mr Wolf's Week* by Colin Hawkins (Heinemann Young Books) and *Weather Watch* in the *I Can Help* series (Franklin Watts).

What to do
Start by printing the words 'Today is' on the computer and positioning the words on the board. Leave space to fit in the day of the week after it. Underneath add the words 'The weather is' and a space for a description of the weather. Print the days of the week and words to describe the weather with pictures onto separate rectangles of brightly-coloured card. Laminate the cards to protect them and to extend the life of your weather chart.

Use the photocopiable sheet to make weather symbols and add these to the corners of the chart.

Encourage the children to sing the following rhyme to the tune of 'Aiken Drum' when carrying out the activity.

'How is the weather, the
weather, the weather,
How is the weather outside today?'.

Teach the children the weather song and explain that each child will have a turn to fill in the weather chart. Go through the words describing the weather. Can the children tell you the sort of weather that each represents? Ask them what the weather is like today and which of the word cards best represents it.

Use the chart to reinforce naming and sequencing the days of the week, morning and afternoon and to develop descriptive language. Let the children take turns to fill in the weather chart.

Talk about
● Discuss different types of weather.
● Talk about how the weather changes with the seasons.
● Ask the children which kind of weather they like best and why.

Home links
● Encourage parents to watch the weather forecast on television with their children to see the weather symbols that are used.
● Suggest that parents make a simple weather chart at home with their children, using a piece of paper and drawing on the symbols.

Use the natural resource of weather to encourage the children to find out about the world around them. Take a look at all types of weather with these colourful displays and discover the effects it has on us every day.

Jack Frost

Learning objectives: to understand that cold turns water to ice and frost; to ask questions about why things happen.

What you need
Stiff backing paper; 'hot and cold' coloured tissue paper; white or silver corrugated card; PVA glue; scissors; foil; paintbrushes; silver card; warm clothing; picture books showing the weather; magnifying glass; silver sequin waste.

What to do
If possible, choose a frosty day to introduce this display so that the children can observe and feel the frost at first hand. Explain that frost is frozen dew and first appears in autumn, marking the end of the growing season.

Look at the fern-like patterns that frost makes on the windows; use a magnifying glass to see the ice crystals. Ask if the children have ever heard of Jack Frost, an imaginary, mischievous chap who paints the windows and covers the land with his icy touch. Explain that you are going to make a collage of Jack Frost together. Ask the children to suggest some cold, icy colours. Tip out a collection of coloured papers and start to sort them, putting blue, purple, grey, silver and white at one end of the table and red, orange, yellow and gold at the other. Can the children identify which set are the hot colours and which are the cold? Where would they place green and brown?

Next, sketch out a spiky Jack Frost shape onto a piece of stiff paper. Make a jagged outline like a many-pointed star. Ask a small group of children to cover the Jack Frost shape with watered-down PVA glue, painting it on with brushes. Another group can tear up some of the

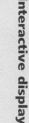
Using the display

Language and literacy
● Think of words to describe Jack Frost and write a class poem.
● Draw spiky zigzag lines and curved wavy lines. Which letters use these shapes?
● Make a collection of silver paper and shiny things. Talk about and compare dull and shiny things.
● Find some pictures of magpies and other birds that collect shiny things.

Mathematical development
● Look at shapes with straight and curved sides.
● Find out which shapes link together or tessellate and which do not. Look at patchwork quilts and mosaics.

Knowledge and understanding of the world
● Put some water outside in a dish on a very cold day (or in a freezer). Observe what happens to it. What will happen if you bring the dish back into the warm room?

● Think about the different seasons and compare the activities we can do outdoors in each season.
● Care for the birds in cold weather; put out food and water for them.
● Think of ways to keep warm in cold weather, such as running around.

Physical development
● Practise making spiky movements to some lively music.
● Do some running and jumping exercises to keep warm on a cold day.

Creative development
● Give each child a coloured paper triangle and ask them to fill it with small collage items such as glitter, matchsticks or sequins. Join them all together to make one large triangle.
● Paint pictures of a cold day using 'cold' colours such as purple, grey and white.
● Make a 'frosty' collage using shiny, silver items such as sweet papers, tinsel, glitter, tin foil and other items sprayed with silver paint.

'cold coloured' tissue paper and a third group can stick it down onto the gluey body. Finish with a wash of glue to make sure that the tissue is well stuck down and to give it a glossy finish.

When the glue is dry, cut Jack Frost out. Make his arms and legs from corrugated white or silver card curved into tubes and stuck down with tape. Cut star-shaped hands and feet from silver card and add a mischievous face.

Back your display board with silver foil, attach a sheet of coloured tissue paper to the centre and place Jack Frost in the middle of the board. Leave the points of his body curling out from the board to add to the 3-D effect.

Make a simple border with lengths of silver sequin waste cut into a zigzag pattern and attach this to the tissue paper edge. Mount the heading 'Jack Frost' on a piece of coloured paper.

Place a display table in front of the board and show items of warm clothing (hat, gloves, scarf) and picture books with pictures of cold, icy weather on it.

Talk about
● Talk about icy mornings when the children are on their way to your group. What do the trees and grass look like?
● What clothes do the children wear when the weather is frosty?

Home links
● Ask parents to encourage their children to look at the windows on a very cold morning, searching for patterns made by the frost.
● Encourage parents to provide their children with some gloves and a hat to wear in the cold weather.

Weather

THEMES ON DISPLAY for early years

Umbrellas

Learning objectives: to learn that protective clothing can keep you dry; to use imagination in art and design.

What you need

Plates with mixed powder paint in assorted colours; sugar paper; newspaper; corks; blue backing paper; a roll of border paper in a contrasting colour; paintbrushes; large and child-size umbrellas; wellington boots; plastic rainhat and raincoat; soft toy doll dressed in rainclothes; *Postman Pat's Rainy Day* by John Cunliffe (Hippo).

What to do

If possible, start this display on a rainy day so that the children can watch the raindrops trickling down the window panes. If appropriate, let the children go outside in their coats and wellington boots to splash in the puddles and feel the rain on their hands and faces. Take a large umbrella with you and let the children group around you to shelter underneath it.

Back inside, cut a large umbrella shape for each child from sugar paper. Cover the painting table with newspaper and ask a child to give out an umbrella shape to each of the children sitting at the table. Provide plates with paint in several colours, brushes and corks.

Laying the umbrella shapes flat on the table, ask the children to paint them all over with one colour or divide them into three and paint each section a different colour. Then they can take a cork dipped into a contrasting colour and print circles on to make patterns. Paint the umbrella handles brown and leave them to dry.

Cover the display board with blue backing paper and select six umbrellas to pin to the board. Put a simple border around the display by using a strip of paper or card in a contrasting colour. Label the display '6 Umbrellas'.

On the display table you could add a pair of wellington boots, a child's umbrella, a plastic rainhat and raincoat, a soft toy or doll dressed in a raincoat and rainhat and some information and story-books about the rain.

OUR WORLD

Talk about
● Disuss good things and bad things about rainy days.
● We wear clothes to keep us warm and dry and to protect our skin from the sun and the wind. Can the children think of other types of protective clothing such as fireproof suits and wetsuits?

Home links
● Ask parents to send their child in with wellingtons and a raincoat ready for a walk in the rain.

Using the display
Personal, social and emotional development
● Look at a variety of clothes and decide which are best for different types of weather.
● Cut out pictures of people from magazines and ask the children to stick them onto backgrounds showing the three main weather types; sunny, rainy, cold.

Language and literacy
● Think of the different words used to describe the rain.
● Learn some rainy day poems such as 'Incy Wincy Spider', 'Dr Foster Went to Gloucester', 'Rain, Rain, Go Away' and 'I Hear Thunder'.

Mathematical development
● Draw some umbrella shapes onto pieces of paper. Ask the children to draw specific numbers of circles onto each one.
● Roll six marbles or small balls down cardboard tubes fixed together or down lengths of clean, plastic drainpipe. Do six come out at the bottom?

Knowledge and understanding of the world
● Go outside on a wet day and watch the water running down the drains – where does it go?
● Look for gutters and drainpipes on buildings. Watch the water running down the roof into the gutters Think about the shape of the roof.
● Draw around a puddle with chalk. What happens to the puddle when the sun comes out?

Physical development
● Put on wellington boots and let the children jump in or over the puddles.
● Let the children use their fingers to show how the raindrops fall from the sky. Start with slow, gentle rain then make the rain fall faster and faster.

Creative development
● Try making 3-D umbrellas with two card umbrella shapes slotted together in the centre and a lolly stick for the handle.
● Make rainy day paintings by dripping water onto your pictures and holding them up so that the water runs down the page.
● Experiment by painting on wet and dry paper. What happens to the paint on the wet paper?
● Make rainsticks using cardboard sweet or crisp tubes. Place plastic or wire mesh inside the tube and let dried peas or lentils run through as the rainstick is tipped upside down and back up again.

Rainbows

Learning objectives: to discover that rainbows are sometimes seen in the sky when the rain falls and the sun shines at the same time; to explore colour, texture, shape and form.

What you need

Two plastic hoops; white and dark blue crêpe paper; gold craft paper; silver card; sticky tape; thread; white card and textured paper; pale blue backing paper; coloured card and paper scraps in red, orange, yellow, green, blue and purple; six sorting trays; a collection of sorting toys in the above colours; Blu-Tack; colour cards from *Nursery Projects* 'Colours' (Scholastic) or other sources; PVA glue; A1 sugar paper; books such as *Colours* by Shirley Hughes (Walker Books), *Maisy's Colour's* by Lucy Cousins (Walker Books) and *Sally's Amazing Colour Book* by Paul Dowling (Anderson Press).

What to do

Cut the crêpe paper into strips. Wind strips of white paper around one hoop and dark blue around the other so that they are completely covered. Cut a circle and ten or more triangles from a selection of gold craft paper and stick these onto card to make a sun. Attach the sun to one side of the dark blue hoop using tape. Cut a cloud from white card, cover it with white textured paper and attach it to the second hoop. Cut eight raindrops from silver card and stick them back-to-back with thread stuck in between so that they can be suspended from the cloud. Make labels with the words 'sun' and 'rain' using letters cut from gold and silver card and then suspend the hoops above the display area. Place the six trays, each labelled with a colour card (red, orange, yellow, green, blue and purple) on the floor or table where the children can play freely with them. Provide sorting toys in the six colours and ask a group of children to sort the toys into the colour trays.

When all the toys have been sorted, ask the children to name the colours. Have they ever seen a rainbow in the sky? Do they know what kind of weather is required to make a rainbow?

Explain that you are going to make a rainbow out of paper. Start by tearing or cutting up coloured paper scraps and

sorting them into trays according to their colour. Draw a large rainbow shape onto two pieces of A1 sugar paper stuck together. Divide the rainbow into sections and show the children where to spread the glue. Stick red paper onto the first section and then continue with one colour at a time until the rainbow is complete.

Cover the display board with pale blue paper and attach the colour cards along the bottom using Blu-Tack to keep them in place. Attach the rainbow to the wall above the cards and place the six sorting trays, one in front of each colour card, on the display table in front. Attach the mobiles so that they hang over the rainbow, one at each end. Cut the letters for the word 'Rainbow' from coloured card, using rainbow colours, and arrange over the rainbow. To finish off the display, position the container of sorting toys nearby. Place a few in each tray to help the children get started and encourage them to sort the toys into the correct trays.

Talk about
● Explain that the colours of the rainbow always appear in the same order. Ask the children to tell you which colour they like best; which is the most popular colour?

Home links
● Make a colour table and ask parents if their children could bring in a contribution of the relevant colour.

Using the display
Personal, social and emotional development
● Use musical instruments to make the sounds of wind, rain and thunder. Play in groups, taking turns to listen to each other.
● Work in groups to make colour mosaics using squares of coloured paper.

Language and literacy
● Listen to some 'weather' sounds made by a variety of objects such as a crisp packet, a triangle, a wood block, a rainstick or a bunch of keys. Play them individually while the children are watching you, then play them behind a screen. Can the children identify each one?
● Tell the story of *Noah's Ark* retold by Lucy Cousins (Walker Books).

Creative development
● Make mobiles out of shiny card shapes and suspend them from the ceiling at different heights.
● Make a wind chime out of metal objects hung where they will knock into each other.
● Provide yellow, blue and red paint for children to mix and make new colours and shades. Encourage them to talk about what colours they are using and what they can see as they mix them together.

Weather

THEMES ON DISPLAY for early years

Kites in the wind

Learning objectives: to understand that wind creates movement; to move with control and co-ordination.

What you need

Sugar paper; scissors; card; powder paints in blue, white and red; brightly-coloured sheets of A4 craft paper; sticky tape; coloured tissue paper; ribbon; PVA glue; circular sponges; a kite; flags; a toy windmill; books such as *The Wind Blew* by Pat Hutchins (Red Fox) and *Windy Day* by Mick Manning in the *Early Worms* series (Franklin Watts).

What to do

Start off by talking about the wind in general and what it feels like to be out on a really windy day.

Ask the children if they can think of any toys that use the wind to make them move. Show them a kite or cut a kite shape out of paper. Explain that you are going to make some paper kites to go on the wall. Have ready some cut-out paper shapes including triangles and ask the children which shapes they think they will need to make the kites.

Fold the A4 craft paper diagonally and cut out to make triangles. Let the children choose two colours for their kite and ask them to take two triangles of each chosen colour and arrange them on the table to make a kite shape. Once the children are happy with their arrangement, help them to stick the triangles together to make the kite. Add a tail made from a long strip of coloured paper or ribbon and squares of tissue paper twisted to make bows. Stick thin strips of coloured paper at the side corners and ask the children to paint a face in the centre of their kite.

For the background, mix up plates of blue and white powder paint and show the children how to create swirls of colour on the sheets of sugar paper using circular sponges. When the backing paper has dried, attach it to the display board adding the children's kites to create the effect of kites dancing in the wind.

Kites

Make a border from a strip of contrasting coloured paper and add a heading 'Kites' written in bold, bright letters on a piece of plain card, ideally mounted on a slightly larger piece in a contrasting colour, and attach to the bottom of the display.

Add kites, flags, windmills, story-books and pictures about the wind to the display table.

Talk about
● Ask the children how we know the wind is there, even though we can't see it.
● Look at the trees and people through the window on a windy day to see what the wind does to them.
● Think of ways that we make use of the wind such as to dry the washing, sail a boat or turn a windmill.

Home links
● Ask the children to bring in something from home for your collection.
● Invite parents to come and help a group of children fly kites.

Using the display
Language and literacy
● Listen to the wind and describe what you hear. Introduce words to describe the different strengths of the wind – gale, breeze and so on.

Knowledge and understanding of the world
● Try drying pieces of material or dolls' clothes in different weather conditions to see which type of weather is the most effective for drying clothes.
● Compare a small plastic figure falling to the floor with a figure attached to a parachute. Which falls faster?
● Blow up a balloon and ask the children what is making it get bigger. If they can't see the air in the balloon how do they know it is there? Let the children feel the air escape from the balloon over their hands.

Physical development
● Try running into the wind and against the wind to see which is the easiest to do.
● Think of ways to make a wind indoors to make paper boats move, such as blowing through a straw or fanning them with a paper fan.
● Let the children feel the strength of the wind by taking turns at helping to hold the kite string as it flies.

Creative development
● Make interesting pictures by blowing ink or thin paint across a page.
● Make some paper fans and feel the air against your face.
● Decorate some paper flags.
● Attach lengths of crêpe paper to garden cane or long paintbrushes. Take them outside and watch them dance in the wind.

Weather

THEMES ON DISPLAY
for early years

Sunny days

Learning objectives: to understand the need to protect self from the sun; to identify and name basic shapes.

What you need

Light blue backing paper; red and yellow powder paint; yellow and orange card; newspaper; PVA glue; scissors; paintbrushes; gold glitter in a shaker; wax crayon; a gold pen; craft papers in orange, yellow and gold; white paper; books such as *Hot and Cold* in the *It's Science* series (Franklin Watts) and *Freddie Goes to the Seaside* by Nicola Smee (Orchard); gold or yellow cloth; a teddy wearing sun-glasses and a sun-hat; sun cream; sun-glasses; sun-hat.

What to do

Introduce the subject by talking about the sun, where it is and what it gives us. Think about the warmth we receive and consider how hot the sun must be.

Explain to the children that they are going to make their own suns using paper and paint. Cover the tables with newspaper and give each child in the group a circle (15cm in diameter) cut from the orange or yellow card. Next, give out pots of red and yellow paint. Show the children how to add some of the yellow to the red and vice versa. Watch as different shades of orange appear. Share the pots around, making sure that you have some red and yellow as well as shades of orange.

Show the children how to dip a brush into the paint and hold it, full of paint, over the paper circle to drizzle onto the paper. The paint needs to be thin enough to drip onto the paper but not watery. Encourage the children to use

several different shades of colour, then let them sprinkle some gold glitter onto the wet paint using a pot with a shaker lid on. Leave to dry overnight.

Cut out plenty of long, thin triangle shapes from orange, yellow and gold craft papers. Ask the children to stick the triangles all around their suns as rays. Show them how to apply glue to the wide ends of the triangles and tuck them under their circles and press down. This is better than turning the sun circle upside-down and risking rubbing the paint off. Next, cover the display board with a light blue paper and attach the sun circles with a staple gun or drawing pins. Use a couple of paper clouds to tuck behind the suns. Give the children pieces of card and a gold pen and ask them to try writing their own 'sun' labels. Let them practise on rough paper with a pencil first. For younger children, draw the letters onto the card with a pencil and let them write over your letters with the gold pen. Use a gold wax crayon to decorate the labels. Add the labels to the display.

Cover the display table with a piece of gold or yellow cloth, add a teddy wearing sun-glasses and a sun-hat, a bottle of sun cream and additional sun-hats and sun-glasses. Add some labels with pictures and the word 'sun' to help the children recognize the word.

Talk about
● Talk about ways to protect ourselves from the heat of the sun such as wearing a sun-hat, using plenty of sun cream and sitting in the shade.
● Think of fun things to do on a sunny day such as having picnics with your friends, going to the beach or setting up a paddling pool in the garden.

Home links
● Ask parents to send in sun-hats and sun cream for their children in the summer.
● Ask some parents to help with a summer picnic for the children.

Using the display
Language and literacy
● Practise writing 's' for sun.
● Think of words that begin with 's' and make a collection of relevant items.

Knowledge and understanding of the world
● Think about ways to make light and make a collection of candles, lanterns and torches.

Physical development
● Play a shape game – put a shape in each corner of the room and tell the children to run to the shapes when they hear the name called. What shapes make up their 'suns'?

Creative development
● Make some summer shape pictures using gummed shapes.
● Use shaped sponges dipped in paint to print colourful pictures.
● Cut shapes from thick card and use as stencils.
● Make a sunny badge with a smiley face to wear.

Weather

THEMES ON DISPLAY for early years

Blow wind blow

Learning objectives: to show that some toys use the wind to make them move; to be confident to try things, initiate ideas and speak in a group.

What you need
A collection of some of the following: windmills, paper fans with diamond shapes cut out and tails of ribbon, sailing boats of polystyrene with plastic straw masts and paper sails, a parachute toy, flags made from coloured paper decorated with gummed paper shapes, a pot of bubbles, wind chimes, paper aeroplanes, a pocket kite; a roll of blue corrugated card; tins and plastic jars; coloured paper; scissors; water tray; straws; clay; paints; paintbrushes.

What to do
Using blue corrugated card as a backdrop, cut the top edge to give it an undulating effect with which you can cover any unsightly areas of wall to make a free-standing table display.

Arrange the collection of toys on the display table at different heights to show them off to their best advantage. Make paper flags out of squares and triangles of different-coloured paper. Decorate them with gummed shapes and display in tins covered with paper.

Try racing the polystyrene boats in a water tray by blowing air through a straw at them.

Make some simple wind chimes using shapes cut out of clay with small holes in the top of each. Paint them when dry and hang them near the window so that they knock against each other in the wind. Label the display.

Let the children stand in front of the group and show what they have brought in from home or made for the display. Encourage them to speak out and describe what they have brought and how it uses the wind. Use the display to teach the children to take care of each other's belongings.

Talk about
● Talk about the way each of the toys uses the wind.

Home links
● Ask the children to bring in a contribution for the display from home.

Further display table ideas
● Make a display of model sailing boats made from polystyrene trays with plastic straws for masts and coloured paper sails. Number the boats from 1 to 10 and place them in a shallow water tray. Provide straws and let the children work in pairs to race the boats.

OUR WORLD

Places

Places we visit

Learning objectives: to find out about the environment, and talk about those features that are liked and disliked; to use talk to organize, sequence and clarify thinking, ideas, feelings and events.

What you need

Photographs of children at the park, in the woods, on the beach, at the pond or other relevant areas; sheets of A3 card in four colours; photo mounts; headings for each area; green, yellow and blue corrugated paper; small-world play people, a swing, slide and trees; small toy ducks; small shells; a tiny toy fish; books such as *The School Trip* in the *Picture Knights* series by Mick Inkpen (Hodder), *Out and About* by Shirley Hughes (Walker Books), *Having a Picnic* by Sarah Garland (Bodley Head) and *Ten Out of Bed* by Penny Dale (Walker Books).

What to do

Using either pictures taken specially for the display or pictures taken on previous outings with your group, select photographs to illustrate four local areas such as the woods, the pond, the beach and the park. Choose four different coloured pieces of A3 card and arrange one collection of pictures on each. Fix in place with photo mounts. Centre them around colourful headings, made using clip art borders, coloured paper or drawn by hand. Attach the montage to a display board with a fixed surface in front. Put the heading 'Places to visit' in the centre and cover the display table with green, yellow and blue corrugated card – cut to represent the wood, the sand and the water. Place the small-world toys and other items onto the card of the appropriate colours. Label each area 'The beach', 'The park', 'The duck pond' or 'The woods'.

Talk about

● Invite the children to talk about the places that they have visited and places that they would like to go to.
● Encourage the children to talk about trips that they particularly enjoyed, and anticipate future events.
● Talk about places that the children go for birthdays or a special treat as well as places that they visit more often, such as the park or the woods.

Home links

● Ask parents to loan photographs of their children taken at local places of interest. Involve them in talking with their children about the places that they went to and what they did there.

Places to visit

The market place

Learning objectives: to investigate objects and materials by using the senses; to recognize the importance of keeping healthy and what contributes to this.

What you need

Rolls of yellow, red and blue backing paper; a thick cardboard box; collage materials; light brown card; tissue paper; black felt-tipped pen; wax crayons; cartridge paper; PVA glue; scissors; powder paints; approximately 3m of dowelling rod; artificial grass or green paper; plastic mushroom boxes; plastic fruit; a toy till; toy money; a balance; pad and pencil; a basket of fresh fruits; small pots; *Handa's Surprise* by Eileen Browne (Walker) and *The Shopping Basket* by John Burningham (Red Fox).

What to do

Start off the session by showing the children a basket filled with as many different fresh fruits as possible. Pass the fruits around the group one at a time and ask the children to try to identify them. Encourage them to use their senses and describe how each fruit looks, feels and smells. Having checked for food allergies, cut up the fruit and encourage the children to taste a small piece of each. Compare the inside with the outside of the fruit and look at the pips, peel and juice. Make small pots of fruit salad to eat at snack time. Can the children still identify the individual fruits?

Put up pale blue backing paper on your display board and then measure out a double thickness from the roll of red and yellow paper to approximately half the width of the area to be covered by the stall. Cut both the red and yellow paper into four strips of about 30cm in width. Open them out and stick the strips together to form a striped canopy. When dry, fold the canopy back in half

The Market Garden

grapes 6p

pineapple 5p

melon 5p   oranges 3p   apples 2p

Using the display
Mathematical development
● Use plastic pennies to buy the fruit in the market.
● Use the balance to develop an understanding of heavier and lighter. Weigh an apple and a melon by hand to feel the difference before placing in the balance.
● Cut up apples and discuss 'whole' and 'half'.

Knowledge and understanding of the world
● Find out which fruits grow in our country and which come from hotter climates.
● Try making orange juice. How many oranges do the children think it will take to make one cup of juice?
● Collect labels from foods containing fruit such as jam, jelly and juice.
● Read *Handa's Surprise* naming the fruits and animals which ate them.

Creative development
● Try painting pictures of a bowl of fruit
● Make some prints using apples cut in half.
● Make fruit from play dough and practise cutting the fruit in half with a plastic knife. Use other tools to draw on pips and patterns.

and staple the open ends to the top of the board and thread a length of dowelling rod or garden cane into the folded end to give it weight. To hold the canopy out from the wall, cut three hinged pieces of cardboard from the corners of a cardboard box, support the canopy with one half of the hinge and staple or pin the other half to the display board.

Make a rough sketch of the stallholder and ask one of the children to paint her in bright colours. Cover the bottom part of the board with artificial grass or bright green paper and make fruit boxes from strips of light brown card overlapping to form rectangles and fill with blue tissue paper and paper fruits.

To make the oranges, cover paper with a thin wash of paint and give it the bumpy texture of orange skin by rubbing wax crayon over a rough surface. Make the melons in the same way, using green paint and crayon and cutting them into larger circles.

The apples are made by covering paper with pieces of red and yellow tissue paper and a seal of PVA glue. For the bunches of grapes, give the children triangular outlines to fill by dipping their index fingers in thick green and purple paint. Cut out pineapple shapes for the children to colour in with wax crayon and show them how to finish with a criss-cross pattern using a black felt-tipped pen. Label the boxes of fruits

with the names and prices.

Fill the display table with plastic boxes and trays filled with play fruit and vegetables. Provide a till, play money, shopping baskets and purses. Add a balance to weigh the plastic fruit and a pad and pencil to write shopping lists.

melon   5p

Talk about
● Talk about the shops and markets that the children have visited.
● Explain to the children about the fruit as part of the plant, which protects the seeds that will grow into new plants.

Home links
● Ask parents to encourage their children to point out and name different kinds of fruit when they go shopping together.
● Suggest to parents that they allow their children to help weigh the fruit in the supermarket.
● Ask the children to bring in a piece of fruit to share for snack time. Make a list of the most popular fruits.

oranges   3p

The pet shop

Learning objectives: to find out about and identify some features of living things; to find out which animals make good pets.

What you need
Paper plates; powder paints; Art Straws; egg boxes; pens; card; blue Cellophane; scraps of green paper; PVA glue; wobbly eyes; red backing paper and blue border roll; craft paper; feathers; coloured card and paper; sand; toy pets; clay; string; gummed paper; the photocopiable sheet on page 75 copied onto card; boxes; plastic containers; books on pet care and stories such as *The Great Pet Sale* by Mick Inkpen (Hodder), *Puppy*, *Rabbit* and *Fish* in the *Me and My Pet* series by Christine Morley (Two-Can) and *Dog Dottington* by Diana Hendry (Walker Books); a vet's kit; soft toy pets.

What to do
Ask the children if any of them have a pet and if so what sort of pets they have. Consider all the pets mentioned and then ask, 'Does anyone have a lion? Why not?'. Use this exchange as a starting point for a discussion on what makes a good pet. Encourage the children to think about the responsibility of owning a pet and looking after it.

Cover the display board with red paper and add a blue border. Place a central heading 'Pets' cut from coloured card letters and the group headings 'cats', 'dogs', 'birds' and 'fish'.

Explain that you are going to make some dogs out of card shapes to put in your pet shop display. Give each child a card photocopy of a dog, ask them to name, cut out and assemble the different shapes, adding spots and a tail using a pen.

To make the cats give each child a paper plate and paint or gummed paper to make the features plus Art Straws for whiskers and card triangles for ears. Discuss where each feature goes as they stick the face together then ask the children to try painting their own pictures of cats.

Use a paper plate with a circle of blue Cellophane in the centre for the fish bowl and torn scraps of green paper for the weed. Give the children pieces of orange paper to draw their own goldfish on or provide cut-out shapes. Spread the glue along the bottom of the bowl and sprinkle some sand on.

The parrot's head, body and feet are cut from thin coloured card which is stuck together and decorated with coloured feathers and long strips of coloured paper.

Using the display
Language and literacy
● Read some stories and poems about pets such as *The Great Pet Sale* by Mick Inkpen or *Dog Dottington* by Diana Hendry.
● Learn rhymes such as 'Hickory Dickory Dock' and 'Pussy Cat, Pussy Cat'.

Mathematical development
● Stand ten card mice in a row and number them from 1 to 10. Take two mice out of sequence and see if the children can work out which of the numbers are in the wrong places.
● Make a simple graph of the children's pets. Which is the most popular?

Knowledge and understanding of the world
● Explain that pets are animals that we care for in our homes, unlike farm or wild animals. Sort animal pictures to check the children's understanding of this.
● Ask the children to find out what each baby animal becomes, for example puppies become dogs.
● Develop role-play ideas using soft toy animals to promote caring for animals.

Physical development
● Move around the room pretending to be different pets.
● Listen to *The Carnival of the Animals* by Saint-Saëns and work out dance and movement ideas, comparing the movement of different animals.

On the display table, place some mice made from clay with string tails and tortoises made from individual egg box sections with wobbly eyes and legs and head cut from card. A dog's kennel and cat's basket can be made from cardboard boxes, and a shoebox makes a good mouse house! The aquarium is a box painted and filled with clay fish and cardboard weed. Plastic containers can be used for pet food. Dog biscuits are cut from circles of thick card. Add a vet's kit and some soft toy pets.

Talk about
● Encourage the children to explain which animal they would like for a pet and why.
● Talk about what makes a good pet. Suggest different animals and ask the children whether they would make good pets or not. List the attributes of a good pet.

Home links
● Invite some parents to help on a visit to a local pet shop.
● Ask some owners and their pets to visit your group (check any health and safety implications).

Interactive display

The woods

Learning objective: to look closely at similarities, differences, patterns and change.

What you need
Bright blue and green backing paper; light green border paper; corrugated paper; powder paints; painting plates; paintbrushes; sponges; sugar paper; PVA glue; a collection of leaves including three contrasting examples such as pine, oak and sycamore; pieces of bark; twigs; a small log; clay; coloured card; craft paper; cardboard tubes; fabric; basket; coloured string; the photocopiable sheet on page 76 (copied onto card); books such as *Harry's Stormy Night* by Una Leavy (Orchard), *Jeremiah in the Dark Woods* by Janet and Allan Ahlberg (Puffin) and *The Wild Woods* by Simon James (Walker Books).

What to do
If possible, take the children outside to collect some fallen leaves. Alternatively, bring in a basket of clean leaves that you have collected yourself. Make sure that the leaves are a variety of shapes, sizes and colours. Some could be old and dry and others newly collected.

Sit the children in a circle on the floor. Tip the leaves into the centre of the group and ask the children to carefully pick up and feel some of the leaves, looking particularly at the shapes, patterns and colours. Cover a table with newspaper and plates of powder paint plus a little water for the children to mix shades of green, brown, orange and yellow. Show the children how to cover the backs of the leaves with fairly thick paint and press them onto sugar paper to make prints. Encourage them to try different leaves and different colours of paint.

Using green and red powder paint, let the children mix shades of brown and paint the corrugated paper with sponges or large brushes. Once dry, cut the paper into rectangles for tree trunks and branches.

Cover the display board with blue and green paper and an orange or red border and arrange the tree trunks on it. Encourage the children to help cut out the individual leaf prints and add these to the display. At the bottom of the picture, add some evergreen firs made from light green card folded in half and cut into rough triangles. Mix up some darker green paint and let the children paint lines across one side of the folded tree using finger-

paint. Now fold the trees in half again and watch as the children open them out to see how the paint has printed onto the opposite side to look like branches. Attach the trees to cardboard painted brown and staple them to the bottom of the frieze so that they stand out.

Cut simple toadstool shapes out of red craft paper and ask the children to stick on a given number of yellow paper spots.

On a fabric-covered table in front of the display, leave a basket of leaves, pieces of bark, fir cones, twigs and a small cut log as well as toadstools made from clay and some card leaves (from the photocopiable sheet on page 76) threaded with coloured string.

Talk about
● Look at pictures of the same trees in different seasons and note how they change.
● Explain that some trees keep their leaves in winter and are known as evergreen.
● Discuss the cyclical pattern of trees growing new leaves, having them change colour in the autumn and fall off and die in the winter.

Home links
● Invite some parents to help on a walk in the woods to look at the trees.
● Encourage the children to look for trees in their gardens and parks and along the side of the road when they are out with their parents.

Using the display
Personal, social and emotional development
● Encourage the children to care for the natural environment by planting a tree and watching it grow.

Language and literacy
● Ask the children to describe the colour, shape and feel of the leaves.
● Listen to and join in with poems about trees. Add sound effects using wood blocks, sandpaper and dried leaves.

Mathematical development
● Make a line of leaves and count each one in turn.
● Make shape trees from triangles and rectangles; count and identify the shapes.
● Grade the leaves from biggest to smallest.
● Match leaves to trees and try to identify some of the leaf shapes.

Creative development
● Using the photocopiable sheet on page 76, encourage the children to colour and cut out some leaf shapes and use them to make collage pictures.
● Make trees out of strips of brown paper and finger print leaves in green, yellow and orange.
● Take rubbings of the leaves with wax crayons and thin paper.
● Print four trees using a stencil and decorate one for each of the seasons.

The duck pond

Learning objectives: to count reliably up to five everyday objects; to say and use number names in order in familiar context; to find one more or one less than a number from one to five.

What you need

Powder paints; green and blue backing paper; pale blue corrugated paper; scissors; shades of green paper; five plastic ducklings and a mother duck; blue and white sugar paper; card; a duck-shaped sponge; paper plates; coloured circles; yellow feathers; a pen; a duck hand puppet; *Five Little Ducks* by Ian Beck (Orchard), *Come on Daisy* by Jane Simmons (Orchard); the rhyme 'Five Little Ducks...' from *This Little Puffin...* compiled by Elizabeth Matterson (Puffin).

What to do

Using a display board at the children's height with a table in front, cover the board with pale blue corrugated paper. Cut a long strip of green paper with hill shapes cut into the top edge and a similar-sized strip of darker blue paper for the pond. Attach it to the bottom half of the display. Help the children to paint and cut out a card pond to put on the display table. Sit a mother duck and five plastic ducklings on the pond.

After looking at pictures of ducks, ask two or three children at a time to paint yellow ducklings and white mother ducks. When these are dry, select and cut out a mother duck and five ducklings to add to the display. Ask another group of children to paint green reeds and rushes in different shades of green and brown. For the sponge-painted ducklings, cut out several small

ponds from blue sugar paper and working with small groups of children, ask them to place the five plastic ducks in a row on the table, then print five ducks onto their first pond using the duck-shaped sponge dipped in yellow paint. Remove one of the ducklings and ask how many are left. Ask the children to print four ducklings onto their second pond. Continue until all the ducks have been removed from the table. When the ponds are dry, ask the children to place them in a line starting with the five ducks and ending with one. Help them to make and stick the correct number label on each pond.

For the hand puppets, fold two paper plates in half and staple half of one plate to half of the other. Cut a third plate in half and staple to the back of one of the other plates to form the duck's head. Paint the inside of the beak orange and the rest yellow. Add coloured circles for eyes and feathers on top of the head. Make the heading '5 little ducks' in large yellow letters cut from card. Teach the children the rhyme, 'Five Little Ducks Went Swimming One Day'.

As you sing the rhyme, remove one duckling at a time from the display, then put them all back again at the end and leave them there ready for the children to use another day.

Talk about
● Talk about the mother duck being brown or white rather than bright yellow. Explain that she is camouflaged so that she can protect her eggs and, later, her ducklings.

● Talk about the ways the ducklings will grow and change as they get older. Look at pictures of male and female ducks to compare their colours.
● Talk about ways to keep safe near ponds and rivers. Use the *Daisy Duck* story to discuss how important it is not to wander off and get lost.

Home links
● Invite some parents to help with a trip to a local pond where the children can feed the ducks.

Using the display
Language and literacy
● Tell the children the story of 'The Ugly Duckling' or stories about *Daisy Duck* by Jane Simmons (Orchard).
● Learn other number rhymes involving the numbers one to five, for example 'Five Little Frogs', 'Five Currant Buns' or 'One, Two, Three, Four, Five, Once I Caught a Fish Alive'.

Mathematical development
● Place the five ducklings on the pond and explain that some are going to hide, then place one or more behind a story-book. Can the children work out how many are hiding?
● Stick numbers on the ducklings from 1 to 5 and see if the children can stand the ducks in numerical order by reading the numbers.

Knowledge and understanding of the world
● Use the water tray or sink and find out which things float and which sink.
● Find out which other creatures might live in the pond.
● Find out the names of other baby animals.

Creative development
● Make some play dough ducks.
● Bake some duck-shaped biscuits.

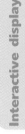

At the beach

Learning objectives: to care for the environment; to handle tools, objects, construction and malleable materials safely and with increasing control.

What you need

Sugar paper; pale blue paper; cartridge paper; newspaper; powder paints; dry sand; white textured paper; scallop shells; a basketful of shells; (do not encourage the children to collect shells themselves); pictures of shells; wax crayons; decorators' brushes; fabric; pebbles; beach toys; books such as *Lucy & Tom at the Seaside* by Shirley Hughes (Puffin), *Magic Beach* by Alison Lester (Allen & Unwin) and *Sally and the Limpet* by Simon James (Walker Books).

What to do

Show the children a basketful of shells and ask them to think about where you might have collected them. Pass some of the shells around for the children to compare and feel. Find some pictures of shells and explain that they were once homes for sea creatures. Read *Sally and the Limpet* and explain the importance of caring for small creatures and putting them back where they came from.

Stress that we should not pick up shells from their natural environments as some are protected by law.

Cover the painting area with newspaper and let the children help to mix up individual shades of blue by adding varying amounts of white or yellow. Cover two or three sheets of sugar paper with overlapping wavy lines for the children to paint in different shades of blue to produce a wavy sea. Cut out and stick on strips of white textured paper for the foam.

Mix up pots of yellow, brown and white paint and ask the children to paint across two or three sheets of sugar paper using decorators' brushes in a stippling movement and blending the colours. Sprinkle a little dry sand onto the wet paint and leave it to dry.

The sky section is made by dragging fingers dipped in blue and white paint across pale blue paper. Make a sun in one corner with swirls of yellow paint. Assemble the three backing sections onto the display board. Then cut out lengths of sugar paper and ask the children to paint themselves freehand or sketch out the outlines for them to paint. Paint other items such as buckets and spades, beach balls, parasols and some crabs.

To make the shells, give a group of children pieces of cartridge paper to wash over with watery-pink or yellow paint. Cut the dried paper into quarters and give a piece to each child in the group. Pass around the scallop shells and show the children how to position the shell under the cartridge paper and rub over the surface with a wax crayon. Attach the finished 'shells' to the display.

Cover the display table with a plain piece of fabric and add the basketful of shells, large pebbles, beach toys and books about the seaside. Label some of the items.

Add a heading 'At the beach' in bold letters to the top of the display.

Talk about
● Talk about visits to the seaside and keeping safe at the beach.
● Talk about and look at pictures of creatures that live in rock pools.

Home links
● Ask the children to bring in beach toys to add to the display table.

Using the display
Personal, social and emotional development
● Make sand pies for each other using a tea set and baking trays. Wash up in a bowl of soapy water and provide cloths to dry with.
● Discuss safety rules when using the sand, encouraging children to think of kindness to others.

Language and literacy
● Cut out letters from sandpaper for the children to feel with their fingers. Try writing the same letters on paper with big wax crayons.
● Use sand to make patterns and letter shapes. Show the children how to smooth over the sand and try again.
● Let the children help with list-keeping by sticking a smiley face sticker next to their name on a class chart, showing when they have had a turn in the sand. Use pictures as well as words for the activities.

Mathematical development
● Explore the idea of capacity by filling different-sized containers with sand.
● Sort shells into sets according to size or colour.
● Use the shells or painted pebbles to count with; make rows of five and match with number cards.

Knowledge and understanding of the world
● Bring in some garden snails for the children to observe. Talk about sea creatures that live in shells.
● Compare trays of wet and dry sand. Try building, sieving and pouring with wet and dry sand using funnels, wheels and beakers.

Creative development
● Cover large pebbles with paint, adding spots or stripes in contrasting colours. Varnish when dry.
● Make sand-castles of different shapes and sizes and decorate with shells and home-made flags.

Made from wood

Learning objectives: to find out about, and identify features of objects they observe; to investigate objects and materials by using all the senses, as appropriate.

What you need

Thick sheets of yellow, brown, light and dark green card; items made from wood such as a spoon, a rolling pin, a toy train, toy furniture, a ruler, animals; card for labels; cream card to cover table; sticky tape; sandpaper; wood; bag; metal objects; wooden and metal instruments.

What to do

For the background to the display, fold two A1 pieces of yellow card in half vertically and stick them together with tape so that they stand up in a concertina fashion. Cut the top edge into a wave-like pattern. Using brown card for the trunks and different shades of green for the treetops and leaves, cut out four similar tree shapes and ask a group of children to help stick one tree onto each section of the background card, making each tree slightly different.

Make stand-up card labels for each item. Cover the table with a piece of cream-coloured card, place the trees at the back and add wooden items and labels to the table and the heading 'Wood' at the front of the display.

Invite the children to feel the contrast between rough bark and some smooth polished wood. Provide a piece of sandpaper and show them how to sand down a piece of wood. Put some wooden and metal objects into a bag to see if the children can feel the difference. Try playing wood and metal instruments to see if the children can hear the difference in sound.

Talk about

● Talk about the uses of wood; for building, furniture and for fuel.
● Talk about acorns, conkers, nuts and fruits that grow on trees.
● Discuss and compare some of the different materials around us such as wood, metal and plastic. Look for examples of each in your setting.

Home links

● Encourage the children to look for wooden things in their homes and bring something in for the display.

Further display table ideas

● Make a discovery display using the senses. Provide pieces of wood and sandpaper for the children to work with, items of smooth and rough wood to feel and different-coloured and scented woods. Add a box of sawdust and wood shavings and wooden instruments for the children to play.

Homes

Building homes

Learning objectives: to discover what homes are made of; to be interested, excited and motivated to learn.

What you need

Orange, blue, white and black card; toy diggers and trucks; play people builders; corrugated card or coloured paper in brown and yellow; Blu-Tack; pictures of builders and diggers; sand; Duplo bricks; a play builder's hat; a sand tray; books such as *Digger* by Chris Oxdale in the *Take it Apart* series (Belitha Press) and *Building Site* by Carole Watson in the *Busy Places* series (Franklin Watts).

What to do

For the backdrop, take a large piece of blue card and stick a large semicircle of orange card onto the bottom half to represent the sunset. Add building outlines cut from black card. Attach a strip of orange card to the top of the backdrop. Cut out the letters for 'Building homes' from black card and stick these down with the first word on the orange card and the second word on the blue. Attach to the wall with Blu-Tack.

Place a table in front and cover it with brown and yellow corrugated card cut into sections with wavy edges to represent earth and sand and keep this in place with Blu-Tack. Onto this surface, place some toy diggers, trucks, clean play sand, Duplo bricks, a child's builder's hat and some play people. Add simple labels and attach laminated pictures of diggers, trucks and builders to the front of the table.

Ask the children what they think the workers are going to build. Set up a sand tray next to the display and invite small groups of children to play at being builders in the sand tray. Ask them to explain what they have made and how they built it. Invite a second group to play with trucks and bricks on the floor.

Talk about

● Talk about the different tasks involved in building a house; bricklaying, plastering, painting and so on.
● Talk about diggers, bulldozers and cranes and how they are used on the building site.

Home links

● Ask the children to bring in a toy digger or a crane from home.
● If one of the children's parents works in the construction business, ask if they could come in and show the children some of the hand tools that they use for bricklaying or carpentry.

Learn to select the most appropriate materials to build a home, find out that some animals have their homes under ground and explore what makes our houses homes while creating some wonderful displays in this chapter.

The three little pigs

Learning objectives: to find out which materials make the strongest house; to select the tools and techniques needed to shape, assemble and join the materials being used.

What you need
Powder paints; sugar paper; lolly sticks; Art Straws; sand; PVA glue; rectangular and circular printing sponges; oddments of collage materials; green crêpe paper; building bricks; straw; the story of 'The Three Little Pigs' (Traditional).

What to do
Read the story of 'The Three Little Pigs' to the children. Look at the three building materials mentioned: straw, sticks and bricks. Let the children feel each material and ask them to tell you which material they think is the strongest and why.

To make the houses, cut three identical house shapes from sugar paper. Cover the first with Art Straws and real straw for the roof. Cover the second with lolly sticks stuck in patterns and paint them brown once the glue

has dried. For the third house, paint the sugar paper all over and then print on it with rectangular sponges dipped in reddish paint to make a brick pattern. Paint the roof using brown powder paint mixed with PVA glue and a little sand and ask the children to apply it by dipping their fingers in the mixture and painting onto the roof area with them. This mixture will be thick and as it dries quite quickly, ask several children to apply it at once. Leave to dry on the work table overnight as it is heavy and may break if lifted while wet.

Ask the children to paint individual pictures of the pigs and the wolf, then cut out three of the pigs and a wolf to add to the display. Sponge-paint four A1 sheets of sugar paper with circular sponges using white and blue powder paint to make the sky. Cut the grass from plain green sugar paper decorated with crêpe paper cut into zigzags along the bottom of the picture. Cut out paper flowers and add these to the grass for extra colour. Label the houses 'straw', 'wood' and 'brick' and add the heading 'The 3 Pigs'.

On the display table, add a brick, some straw, Art Straws, wooden lolly

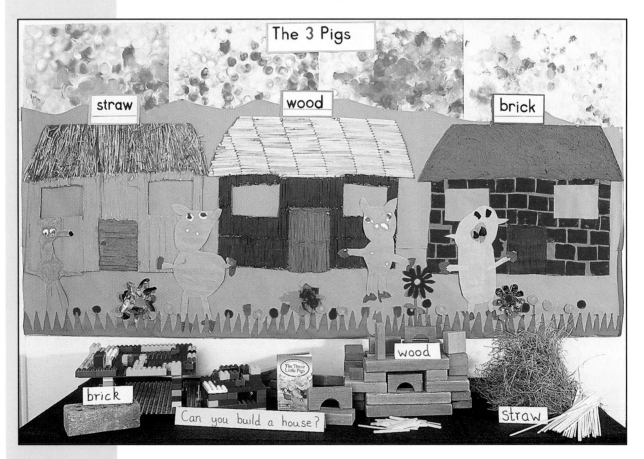

Using the display
Language and literacy
● Make paper-plate pig masks and act out the story of 'The Three Little Pigs'.
● Can the children recall individual events in the story?
● Draw and photocopy pictures from the story. Cut them into sections and ask the children to sequence the events in the story. What happened first?

Mathematical development
● Investigate the number three. Count out groups of three animals and place them in fields drawn on paper.
● Help the children to develop an understanding of first, second and third as you tell the story. Line up three toy pigs and ask which is first. Move him to the end of the line and ask which is first now. Do the same with a line of children.
● Make pig faces using cut out shapes: a circle for the face, triangles for the ears and so on.

Knowledge and understanding of the world
● Find out which materials are strongest: paper, wood, straw or brick. Build simple houses using these materials and try to blow them down.
● Find out which houses would let the rain in. Try sprinkling water out of a toy watering can over the houses.

Physical development
● Play 'What's the time, Mr Wolf?', running away when the wolf calls 'lunch time'.
● Mime the actions to the story.
● Move around the room like different animals: run like a mouse, walk like an elephant and so on.

sticks, a pile of wooden building bricks and a pile of Duplo bricks. Add a label for each and one that reads 'Can you build a house?'.

Encourage the children to come and try using the simple materials to build a house.

Talk about
● Why couldn't the wolf blow down the house of bricks? Make a simple wall and try blowing it down.
● Where is the best place to build a house? Try building on different surfaces to focus on the idea of a firm foundation.
● What is the best way to build with bricks? Try different ways and see which is the strongest method.

Home links
● Explain to parents that the children are to going to see if they can blow their own homes down!
● Ask parents to discuss safety in the home with their children.

Over ground, under ground

Learning objectives: to learn that some animals live under the ground; to find out about, and identify some features of living things.

What you need
Powder paints; PVA glue; blue, green and brown backing paper; Art Straws; clay; pencils; scissors; staplers; craft matchsticks; craft papers and card; egg boxes; black fabric scraps; wood shavings; twigs; moss; leaves; feathers; card leaf templates; the photocopiable sheets on pages 77, 78 and 79; newspaper; cotton wool; sponge; books such as *Hoot* by Jane Hissey (Hutchinson), *Squirrels* by Brian Wildsmith (OUP), *After the Storm* by Nick Butterworth (Collins), *Goodnight Owl* by Pat Hutchins (Bodley Head) and *Mole Moves House* by Elizabeth Buchanan (Macdonald Young Books).

What to do
Cover the top half of the display board with blue paper, the middle with green, and the bottom with brown paper, adding tunnels using black paint.

Start off with a story such as *After the Storm* in which Percy the park-keeper tells how the animals lose their homes when the tree that they live in is blown down in a storm. Explain that you are going to make some of the animals and new homes for them to live in.

Sketch a tree with roots and branches. Ask a group of children to help paint it and another group to cut out leaves from green paper, using card templates. Add it to the centre of the display.

Use the photocopiable sheet on page 77 to make owls. Cut out and join the sections as shown and decorate with feathers. Alternatively, use the top of an egg box for the body and a piece cut from the bottom for the eyes and beak.

Use lumps of clay for the bodies of the hedgehogs with spines made from coloured matchsticks, cut straws or twigs. Paint pictures of hedgehogs using handprints for the spines or cut out simple card hedgehogs using the photocopiable sheet on page 79 and decorate with Art Straws or matchsticks.

Make squirrels from a cut-out shape painted grey. Add a textured effect

Using the display
Personal, social and emotional development
● Learn how to care for wild animals by putting worms back where you found them.
● Remind the children to wash their hands after handling animals, leaves and so on.

Language and literacy
● Use the display to encourage story ideas and language development.
● Use hand puppets for story-telling, making use of books such as *Hoot*.

Mathematical development
● Develop positional language, such as 'over' and 'under'.
● Compare the size of the animals in real life. Which would be the biggest/ smallest?

Knowledge and understanding of the world
● As you place each animal onto the display ask the children where it lives and place it in the correct part of the picture.
● Find out which animals in the display would sleep through the winter or hibernate.
● Make a simple wormery for the children to see how the worms make tunnels and mix up the soil.
● Find out which animals come out at night-time and which in the daytime. Introduce the word 'nocturnal'.

Physical development
● Collect pictures of wild animals from calendars for the children to cut out and stick.
● Dig tunnels in the sand-pit or put earth in the sand tray for the children to dig in.
● How do the children think that the animals dig under the ground when they can't see where they are going. Try doing things with your eyes shut and discover that the sense of touch is very important when you cannot see. What other senses might you use?

Creative development
● Bring in some snails to look at and make some out of play dough.
● Encourage imaginative play with the play tunnel. Pretend you are a rabbit in his burrow or a mole tunnelling along under the grass.
● Explore the idea of camouflage by making animals out of brightly-coloured paper or paint and putting them against a green or brown background.

using crumpled newspaper dipped into darker grey paint. Make the tails from wood shavings stuck on with PVA glue.

The fox is made from folded sugar paper painted with a sponge.

The rabbits are made from brown paper, using the template on the photocopiable sheet on page 78. Add a cotton wool tail.

Snails are easily made from a length of card curled and stapled to a contrasting coloured body shape.

The moles are made using the template on the photocopiable sheet on page 79 copied onto thin card and decorated with black fabric.

The birds' nests are made from clay decorated with collected materials, including moss, leaves and twigs pressed in the wet clay.

Talk about
● Discuss how animals protect themselves from extreme weather and from their enemies. Look at where they build their homes to see why they choose those locations.
● Talk about how having fur or feathers and living under ground, in a nest or under the leaves, protects wild animals from the cold.
● Talk about the food that wild animals eat and where they find it.

Home links
● Ask parents to help with a nature walk to look for signs of wild animals in the local environment.
● Suggest that parents encourage wild birds into their garden by hanging a nut feeder outside.

The gingerbread house

Learning objectives: to retell narratives in the correct sequence drawing on the language patterns of stories; to use imagination in art and design.

What you need

A large cardboard box; two small dolls; biscuit-coloured sugar paper; scissors; gummed paper circles; small gummed shapes; a small box; two corks; black paint; sugar strands; lolly sticks; card circles; pens; glue; sticky tape; green backing paper; white bubble paper; coloured card; powder paints; green paper scraps; circular sponge; clay tiles; the photocopiable sheet on page 80; *Hansel and Gretel* by Val Biro (OUP).

What to do

Read the story of *Hansel and Gretel* to the children and look together at the pictures of the gingerbread house. What is it made of? Explain that you are going to make your own gingerbread house out of a large box.

Open the top flaps to form the roof and cover the whole box with biscuit-coloured sugar paper. Show the children how to make lollipops with card circles, gummed paper and lolly sticks. Cut a pile of gummed circles in half and demonstrate to the children how to arrange them on the roof to make an overlapping pattern of tiles. Ask a child at a time to choose two colours and help them to stick the gummed circles along the bottom edge of the roof in a repeating pattern. Invite a second child to choose different colours and to stick them overlapping the first line. Continue until the roof is covered with 'tiles'. Use a small box covered with sugar strands and two corks for the chimney.

Cover the display board with green paper, cut out a house shape from biscuit-coloured sugar paper and a roof cut from white bubble paper. Paint two trees onto sugar paper with leaves made from torn green paper. Cut the excess paper from between the branches so that the house shows through. Decorate both houses with 'biscuits' made from circular sponge prints, gummed paper shapes and lollipops. Display the 3-D house in front of the display board with dolls to represent Hansel and Gretel and some painted clay tiles around the house. Use coloured card to cut out the letters for the heading and display the books.

Talk about

● Ask the children to help you retell the story in the correct sequence.
● Think of other fairy-tale homes belonging to giants, witches and other characters.
● Talk about the differences between our homes and the gingerbread house. What would happen to the gingerbread house if it rained?

Home links

● Encourage parents to read fairy-tales to their children by providing books for them to borrow.

Using the display

Personal, social and emotional development
● Discuss stranger danger – never go with a stranger or take sweets from someone you don't know.
● Talk about taking care of your teeth – brushing them regularly, eating good food and visiting the dentist. Make a healthy house using pictures of fruit and vegetables cut from magazines.

Mathematical development
● Using the photocopiable sheet on page 80, ask the children to identify, colour and count the shapes on the gingerbread house. They can use a repeating pattern to colour the roof tiles.
● Continue working on repeating patterns using beads, cotton reels and so on.
● Try folding and cutting a range of other shapes in half and rejoining two halves of different colours.
● Have a shape table where children can sort shapes into labelled trays.

Knowledge and understanding of the world
● Discuss the difference between fact and fiction. Is Hansel and Gretel a true story or just pretend? Is the Queen a real person who lives in a palace in London?

Physical development
● Make trails to follow using bricks – follow the red bricks to find a surprise.
● Try making a treasure hunt with simple clues to follow.
● Give each child a card lollipop to play a game of following instructions – hold your lollipop up over your head, behind your back, under your chin and so on.

Creative development
● Print repeating patterns using a variety of odds and ends with interesting shapes: try cotton reels, corks, Duplo bricks and so on.
● Use some spare lollipops for a shop in the home corner.
● Act out the story, letting the children dress up and take turns at being the different characters.

Homes

THEMES ON DISPLAY for early years

My home

Learning objectives: to learn the names of the rooms and furniture in a house; to extend vocabulary, exploring the meanings and sounds of new words.

What you need

Assorted pieces of thick, A3 coloured card; smaller pieces of card for the furniture; sticky Velcro squares; pens; a dolls' house and furniture (four shoeboxes stuck together can be used to make a simple dolls' house); a family of dolls; a set of furniture templates or pictures of furniture cut from catalogues; books such as *Oh no, Peedie Peebles!* by Mairi Hedderwick (Red Fox), *Homes and Houses* (Usborne), *Moving House* by Anne Civardi (Usborne) and *Moving* by Michael Rosen (Viking).

What to do

Choose four different colours of A3 card, one for each of the four rooms in the house. Draw a line across each of the rooms to show where the floor ends and the wall begins. Make a roof from two triangles of cream or brown card. This provides the basic house shape ready to fill with furniture.

Using the furniture templates, cut out the furniture from coloured card and laminate each piece. Make card labels and laminate these for each of the rooms. Attach sticky Velcro squares to the back of each piece and to the rooms. If you do not have templates, cut suitable pictures from catalogues. Fix the house to the display board without the room names or the furniture.

Set up the dolls' house on a table in front of the display with all the furniture around it. Tell the children that a new house has been built with four rooms. Show them the display house and ask them what each room should be.

Ask the children to name some of the rooms in a house. Which do they think are the most important rooms and why? Continue asking questions then place the names on each of the rooms.

Pick up and name each item of furniture in turn and ask questions such as, 'Does the bath go in the kitchen?' and so on until all the pieces have been placed in the correct positions.

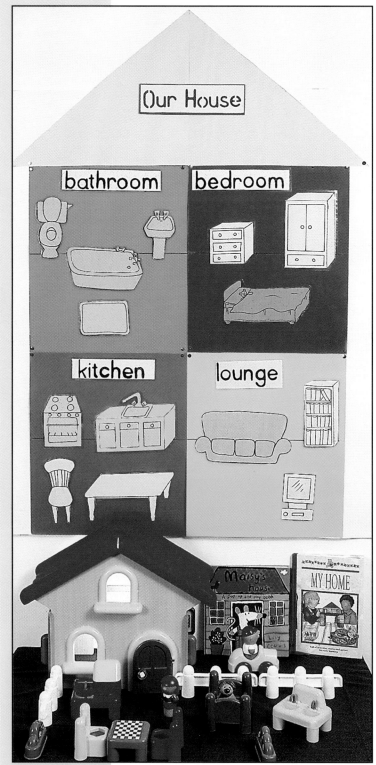

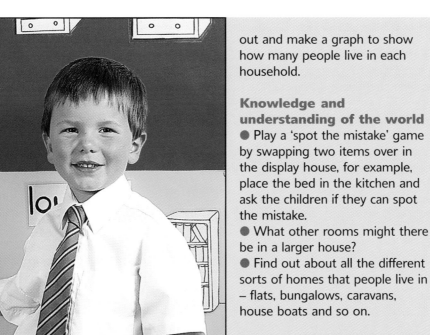

out and make a graph to show how many people live in each household.

Knowledge and understanding of the world
● Play a 'spot the mistake' game by swapping two items over in the display house, for example, place the bed in the kitchen and ask the children if they can spot the mistake.
● What other rooms might there be in a larger house?
● Find out about all the different sorts of homes that people live in – flats, bungalows, caravans, house boats and so on.

Physical development
● Use carpet squares or plastic tiles for a game of colour recognition. Place each colour in a different area of your room, encourage the children to run in and out of the tiles and then run to stand by a named colour.

Creative development
● Give a group of children rollers and printing sponges and ask them to design some wallpaper for the home corner.
● Stick coloured labels on empty cans, thread string handles through holes punched in the top and use them with big clean paintbrushes for role-playing decorators.
● Cut out squares of coloured paper and make a large paint chart for the 'decorators' – use it to reinforce colour recognition.
● Make a card family to live in the display house.

Using the display
Language and literacy
● Read *Oh no, Peedie Peebles!* in which the family move house and paint each room a different colour. Can the children remember which colour was chosen for each of the rooms?
● Ask the children to describe their own bedrooms. What colour are the walls? Are the curtains patterned or plain? Do you share a bedroom or is it just for you?

Mathematical development
● How many people live in your home? Use play people to count with or ask the children to draw the members of their household, cut them

Look at the dolls' house furniture and see if the children can name each piece. Give two children the task of placing the furniture in the dolls' house.

Find a family of dolls who could live in the house and allow the children to play with the house in pairs.

Talk about
● Encourage the children to describe their own homes. What is the name of the room that they eat in? What rooms do they like to play in? Why?
● Ask the children about the room that they sleep in. What colour are the walls and so on.

Home links
● Ask parents for scraps of wallpaper left over from decorating. Can the children tell the rest of the group which room the paper was used to decorate?

Homes

THEMES ON DISPLAY for early years

A view from the window

Learning objectives: to develop skills of observation and recall; to use talk to organize, sequence and clarify thinking, ideas, feelings and events.

What you need
Powder paints; newspaper; pencils; scissors; A3 sheets of sugar paper; A3 sheets of card; coloured tissue; gummed paper; collage scraps; terracotta-coloured sugar paper.

What to do
Take the children to look out of the window together. Ask them to describe what they can see and encourage them to come up with some different answers. Then sit the children down around you and ask what they would like to see out of their bedroom window if they could choose. Help them with various suggestions if they are unsure such as a farm full of animals, the sea crashing on the cliffs, a train puffing over a bridge or a garden full of flowers. Ask them to describe their imagined view.

Cover the painting tables with newspaper and provide plenty of pots of paint in a wide assortment of colours. Using large sheets of sugar paper ask the children to sketch out their imaginary pictures with a pencil and then encourage them to fill the entire piece of paper with colour so that none of the paper can be seen. Allow plenty of time to complete the paintings. These are better done on a table-top rather than an easel so that the paint doesn't run down the page.

While the paintings are drying, cut frames for the pictures from card or thick paper. Mount the children's pictures on the wall and position the window frames over.

Give each child a selection of coloured tissue and sticky paper circles, plus other oddments of collage materials, and explain that you are going to make flowers to put in window-boxes underneath their windows. Let them each make their own or work in pairs.

Cut boxes to fit the length of the window frames from sugar paper in a colour as near to terracotta as you have available. Fill the boxes with the paper flowers and leaves and attach under the windows for a very effective display.

Write a heading on coloured card and display beneath the window-boxes.

Talk about
● Think about how views change as you look out of the car or bus window.
● What happens to the view from an aeroplane as you get higher and higher? Why does everything start to look smaller and smaller?

OUR WORLD

● Talk about living in different places and seeing different views from the window. Read *The Town Mouse and the Country Mouse* retold by Bernadette Watts (North South).

Home links
● Ask some parents if they might like to come and help groups of children to try growing some plants in pots on the window-sill.

Using the display

Personal, social and emotional development
● Show each child's painting to the rest of the group to develop their self-esteem and encourage them to have pride in their work.
● Encourage the children to each talk about their pictures.

Mathematical development
● Develop the idea of distance – far and near. Relate this to why houses and trees look so small when you are in an aeroplane.
● Look at the different-shaped windows in your local environment.

Knowledge and understanding of the world
● Think about the different views seen by children living in different parts of the country. What would you see if you lived in the town, on a farm, by the sea, in the country?
● Would you have a different view if you lived at the top of a block of flats rather than on the ground floor?
● Look at the view out of the windows and play I-spy.

Creative development
● Make some stained glass windows by making tissue paper designs and sticking them onto greaseproof paper.
● Make some viewers with coloured Cellophane attached to the end of cardboard tubes with elastic bands. Describe what you see.
● Mime cleaning the windows with an imaginary bucket of water and a cloth.

Sugar and spice

Learning objectives: to select the tools and techniques needed to shape, assemble and join materials.

What you need
Six shortbread biscuits per house; icing sugar; foil; stiff card; small sweets; a bowl; wooden spoon; a sieve; a blunt knife; *Hansel and Gretel* by Val Biro (Oxford University Press).

What to do
Demonstrate to the children how to mix icing sugar with water, starting with a thin, watery consistency and adding more sugar until you have a consistency that is thick enough to stick the biscuits together. Give each child six biscuits and show them how to spread the icing onto the edges of the biscuits to stick them together. Give each child a small cake board (stiff card) covered in foil and help them to stick their house to the board with icing to prevent it from falling over. Stick four biscuits together to make the walls then add the last two biscuits as a flat roof. Spread icing onto the roof and decorate with or small sweets. Dust the houses with icing sugar to give a snowy effect.

Experiment with more elaborate houses if the children are ready for an extra challenge. Extend by trying to follow simple recipe cards or pictures to sequence the steps taken to make the biscuit houses.

Talk about
● Discuss the importance of washing your hands before preparing food and following simple hygiene rules.
● Are our homes held together with icing? What would happen if they were? Compare bricks and cement with biscuits and icing sugar. Find out which is stronger by trying to break a brick and then a biscuit.

Home links
● Ask some parents to come in and help bake biscuits for the children to take home and share with their families.
● Let the children take their biscuit houses home as a present for a friend or relative. Discuss the importance of giving to other people.

Further display table ideas
● Make a 'healthy eating house' by covering a box with pictures of fruit, vegetables and healthy food cut from magazines. Discuss the importance of healthy eating. Add baskets of plastic fruit and vegetables, books on healthy eating and living, plus books such as *I Eat Fruit* and *I Eat Vegetables* from the *Things I Eat* series by Hannah Tofts (Zero to Ten).

Journeys

How we travel

Learning objectives: to understand the term 'journey'; to use language to imagine and recreate roles and experiences.

What you need

Vehicle stencils; stencil paper; poster paints; stencil brush; a piece of A1 light blue card; scissors; computer clip art pictures of vehicles or magazine pictures; a toy car, bus, train and boat; card labels written for each item; Blu-Tack; a large piece of dark blue cloth; toy suitcases; books on journeys such as *Edward's First Night Away* by Rosemary Wells (Walker Books) or *Going on a Plane* by Anne Civardi (Usborne).

What to do

Use the vehicle stencils to make a set of vehicles to include a bus, a train, a car, a plane, a rocket and a boat. Make stencil pictures using poster paint and a stencil brush. When dry, cut out and arrange the pictures onto a piece of paper, mounted onto light blue card. Add further pictures of vehicles printed from clip art or cut from magazines.

Write or print out the word 'Journeys' and position this behind an aeroplane picture so that it appears as if the sign is being pulled along. When you are satisfied with the arrangement, stick all the pictures into place.

Position the backdrop of stencilled pictures onto a table so that it leans against the wall and hold it in place with Blu-Tack. Cover the table with the dark blue fabric and arrange the toy vehicles on it, placing a label by each. Add books about travelling and a couple of toy suitcases.

Let the children use the stencils to make their own pictures and add these to the display.

Talk about
● Talk about different forms of transport and ask the children which they have travelled in.
● Ask the children to describe their journey to the group, thinking about the things that they passed on the way and the route that they took.
● Different journeys need different preparations – suggest various locations and ask the children if they can think what they would need to take.
● Ask the children to pack a bag for teddy and to explain to him where he is going and what the journey will be like.

Home links
● Ask parents to talk through their journey to the group with their child, noticing what they pass and the route that they take.

Look at the world from space and a hot-air balloon ride as well as from a more down-to-earth perspective with these colourful and informative displays.

A journey into space

Learning objectives: to express and communicate ideas, thoughts and feelings by using a widening range of materials; to use language such as 'circle' and 'bigger' to describe the shape and size of solids and flat shapes.

What you need

Corrugated coloured card; backing paper and contrasting border; thin coloured card; glitter; gummed stars; silver card; red and yellow tissue paper; drawing paper; pens; sticky tape; glue; drawing pins; aprons; paintbrushes; marbling inks; a tray or rectangular bowl; children's scissors; newspaper; *Whatever Next!* by Jill Murphy (Macmillan); factual books about space.

What to do

Read *Whatever Next!* by Jill Murphy or another story about an imaginary journey into space. Ask the children what they think space is like and what they would see there. Look at factual books about space and space travel.

OUR WORLD

Ask the children to draw their own pictures of rockets or aliens using pens and paper. Encourage them to use their imagination and draw fantastical creatures with three heads, purple skin or eyes on stalks! Back the drawings and mount them on a display board covered with purple or black paper.

To make the model rockets, give each child a rectangle of corrugated craft paper approximately 20cm x 15cm, and a circle of thin card in a contrasting colour approximately 15cm in diameter. Ask the children to name the card shapes, count the sides and corners and compare the curved and straight sides. Show them how to roll the rectangle into a tube, noticing how the two ends are now circular in shape and stick the tube together with sticky tape. Help the children to fold and cut their circles in two. Take one half and show the children how to fold it into a cone. Once they can do this, stick the cone together with tape. Compare the remaining semicircle with the cone to see how its shape changes as you fold it. Glue around the top edge of the tube and attach it to the cone. Once the rockets have dried, decorate them with stars or glitter. Stick triangular fins to the sides and flame trails of red and yellow tissue paper. Attach the rockets to the display with drawing pins.

To make the planets, cover a table with newspaper and fill a deep baking tray or bowl with water to within 2cm of the top. Make sure that the children wear aprons and have their sleeves rolled up. Select two or three colours of marbling inks and add a few drops of each to the surface of the water, swirling them together with the end of a paintbrush. Lay a piece of drawing paper on top of the water, lift it out carefully and leave it to dry. Notice the beautiful colours and patterns that have formed on the paper. When all the children have had a turn, and the paper is dry, use it to cut out circular planets and add them to the display. Add a heading, a few gold stars and a silver card ring around one of the planets.

Talk about
● Ask the children if they would like to travel into space and what they think it would be like.

● Show the children a globe and explain that it is a model of the planet that we live on called Earth. Look at the land and water on the globe and show the children where they live.

Home links
● Ask the children to bring in a rocket or a toy alien from home to add to the display or to show to the other children.
● Ask parents for contributions of junk materials or scraps for collage work.

Using the display
Language and literacy
● Ask the children where they think the rocket is going, where it will land and what might be found there.
● Tell a story of an imaginary journey into space. Ask the children to recall and sequence events from the story.

Mathematical development
● When making the model rockets for the display, try using different-sized rectangles of card so that the rockets are of different lengths and use these for comparison.
● Look at, name and describe the solid shapes used to make the rockets in the display.

Knowledge and understanding of the world
● Develop the children's awareness of the planet that we live on. Look at contrasting pictures of sandy deserts, polar ice caps and rain forests.

Physical development
● To introduce work on distance, ask the children to sit at one end of a hall and roll a ball across the floor. Did the ball reach the other side of the room? How far did it go? Can you make it roll further? Did the blue ball roll as far as the red one? Which one rolled the furthest?

Creative development
● Make some space monsters out of play dough or use potatoes and stick on plastic features.
● Make a moon landscape in the sand tray using toy rockets and plastic monsters.

Interactive display

City tour bus

Learning objectives: to use everyday words to describe position; to ask questions about why things happen and how things work.

What you need
Red craft paper; black pen; glue; sugar paper; powder paints; plastic straws; drawing paper; yellow card; black paper; silver paper or card; scissors; pens; gummed paper; green paper; books such as *The Bus Driver* from the *People Who Help Us* series (Wayland).

What to do
Draw the outline of a large open-topped bus onto red craft paper and cut it out. Write a label saying 'City tour bus' with black pen on yellow card to fit under the bus windows. Add wheels made from black paper with centres cut from circles of silver paper or card.

Ask the children to paint pictures of themselves from the waist up to be cut out and put inside the bus. Give them pieces of sugar paper with a circle drawn on in pencil to show them where to paint their face and what size to make it. Explain that the legs will not be seen from the outside of the bus so they do not need to paint them. When the paintings are dry, cut them out and arrange them inside and on the top of the bus looking out.

Give the children rectangles of drawing paper and plastic straws and show them how to make simple flags for the people in the bus to wave. Show them how to fold the rectangle of paper in half, open it out and cover the paper with glue. Placing the straw on the centre fold, press the two halves together. The flags can be decorated with pens or gummed paper shapes.

Cut out a row of flags from green paper to make a simple border.

Talk about
● Discuss different road vehicles and their uses such as cars, buses, taxis, motorcycles, bicycles, vans or trucks.
● Ask whether the children have been on a bus. Where did they go? Was it a long or a short journey?

● Have the children ever been upstairs on a bus and looked out at the view?

Home links
● Ask the children to bring in a toy vehicle from home for the display or to show to the other children.
● Invite some parents to help take the children on a bus ride or maybe visit the local bus depot.

Using the display
Language and literacy
● Using a story like *Rosie's Walk* by Pat Hutchins (Picture Puffin) describe the events of the journey, discussing the main points and introducing the idea that a story has a beginning, a middle and an end.
● Plan a journey with a beginning, middle and an end.
● Sequence a journey using pictures and working from left to right.

Mathematical development
● Number a set of toy vehicles using sticky labels. Line them up in numerical order and count them. Jumble them up and ask the children to reorder them.
● Recognize numerals and realize their value by putting six cars in a row, asking a child to throw a dice and take that number of cars from the row. What number have you thrown? How many cars should you take? How many are left?
● Try again with 20 cars and invite two children to play together. Who has the most cars at the end?

Knowledge and understanding of the world
● How far and fast do wheels roll? Tie a piece of string with a weight on the end to a toy bus. Put the bus on the table with the weight hanging over the edge. What will happen when you let go of the bus? What would happen with a heavier weight?
● Pull a toy bus along the floor with string. Find out whether it is easier to pull when the bus is full or empty. Try pulling the bus along on carpet and lino to see which is easier.
● Roll vehicles down a slope made with a plank of wood. Ask the children to guess where the bus will stop. What will happen if you increase the angle of the slope? Does it make a difference?

Physical development
● Sing 'The Wheels on the Bus' using all the actions.
● Make a bus by placing chairs in rows. Go on an imaginary journey together, going over bridges, through tunnels, noticing landmarks along the way and waving to people out of the windows.

Creative development
● Make buses from card with wheels that turn on paper fasteners.
● Make toy telescopes and binoculars from cardboard tubes. Use them for role-play, looking out to sea, looking at the moon and watching birds.

Let's go fishing

Learning objectives: to explore colour, texture, shape, form and space in two and three dimensions; to use language such as 'more' or 'less', 'greater' or 'smaller', 'heavier' or 'lighter'; to compare two numbers or quantities.

What you need

A1 sheets of blue card or paper; decorator's brushes; sugar paper; newspaper; powder and poster paints; painting plates; washing-up liquid; plastic straws; PVA glue; sequins; clay; small painting sponges; blue corrugated card or blue fabric; brightly-coloured craft paper; books such as *Come Away from the Water, Shirley* by John Burningham (Red Fox), *The Big Big Sea* by Martin Waddell (Walker Books), *The Whale's Song* by Dylan Sheldon (Red Fox) and *The Rainbow Fish* by Marcus Pfister

(North South Books); pictures and models of fishing boats; the children's model fish,

What to do

Cover a painting table with newspaper and four sheets of pale blue card. Using plates of light blue and white paint, show the children how to paint the sky by dabbing small sponges over the surface, keeping some areas all white for clouds. Leave the sheets to dry, then pin them to the top of the display board. Using a fairly stiff decorator's brush, with hard bristles, paint the waves using the same paint, working across the paper with wide wave strokes. Cut the top edge of the paper along the wavy lines and pin the paper to the display board underneath the sponged sky.

Show the children the pictures and models of fishing boats and provide them with A3-sized sugar paper on which to paint their own fishing boats. Select one of the children's boats to add to the display.

For the bubble-painted fish, fill the bottom of a paint pot with 1cm of washing-up liquid, one tablespoon of powder paint and a little water. Ask two children to mix red and blue paint, then give each of them a clean plastic straw and ask them to put the straw down to the bottom of the pot and blow. Make sure that the children understand they have to blow, not suck, or they will have a mouthful of paint!

Once the bubbles have risen over the top of the pot, take a print by placing a piece of paper on top. Let all of the children use the bubble paint, making sure that they have a clean straw each time and that the table is well covered with newspaper.

Draw fish shapes onto the back of the paper and cut out. Give each fish a sequin for an eye or a dab of paint. Make other fish using paint-splattered craft paper and children's handprints.

At the bottom of the display, attach a role of blue corrugated card or a length of blue fabric that can cover a cupboard, book rack or two empty grocery boxes. Onto this extension to the display, you can add toy fishing boats, plastic fish, books about the sea and model fish made by the children from clay or papier mâché.

A Fishing Trip

Talk about
● Talk about types of boats and their uses such as sailing boats, cargo ships, ferry boats and submarines.
● Explain how lifeboats and lighthouses help sailors.

● Find out about the different creatures that live in the sea.

Home links
● Ask the children to bring in a toy fish or boat for the display.

Using the display
Personal, social and emotional development
● Give pairs of children large pieces of drawing paper and encourage them to work together to produce a sea picture. Encourage them to share their ideas as well as the crayons.
● Read *The Rainbow Fish* and discuss giving and receiving.
● Set up a washing area where the children can wash plastic cups and pans. Provide a bowl of warm, bubbly water, dishcloths and drying-up cloths.

Mathematical development
● Provide different-sized containers, jugs and funnels and encourage the children to find out which containers hold the most water.
● Learn some rhymes such as 'One, Two, Three, Four, Five, Once I Caught a Fish Alive' from *This Little Puffin...* compiled by Elizabeth Matterson (Puffin).

Knowledge and understanding of the world.
● Find out which materials change state in water. Investigate which materials are suitable for floating and try making boats out of them.
● See if the boat can carry a play person from one side of the water tray to the other.
● Explore ways of moving the boats across the water with straws, pumps and tubes.
● Turn the water tray into a fish pond with plastic fish, nets and rods.

Physical development
● Fill a bowl or small paddling pool with water and let the children catch toy fish. Catch foam fish with a circle of foam threaded onto a piece of string.
● Play magnetic fishing using small circular magnets taped to string for the rods and card fish with paper clips on. Draw letters or numbers onto the backs of the fish.

THEMES ON DISPLAY
for early years

Up, up and away

Learning objectives: to develop an understanding of 'high' and 'low' and other positional language; to look closely at similarities, differences, patterns and change.

What you need
Marbling inks; a shallow water tray; paintbrushes; powder paints; cartridge paper; white textured paper; doilies; cotton wool; coloured paper cut into 1cm squares; corrugated paper; greaseproof paper; pens; newspaper; PVA glue; a round balloon; string; a small basket approximately 6cm in diameter; two small dolls approximately 6cm tall; a large button; yellow paper; a balloon-shaped template; blue backing paper; red border roll; books such as *Up and Up* by Shirley Hughes (Red Fox) and *Mrs Jolly's Brolly* by Dick King-Smith (Macdonald Young).

What to do
To make the marbled paper, fill a shallow water tray almost to the top with water, add a few drops from two or three different-coloured marbling inks and swirl them together with the end of a paintbrush. Take prints by laying cartridge paper onto the surface of the water and removing them to dry. To make the splattered paper, cover the floor with newspaper and flick paint onto sheets of paper with a paintbrush

Ask the children to choose a sheet of marbled or paint-splattered paper and cut out a balloon shape using a template. Let the children choose their own way of making clouds for their pictures using textured paper, doilies, cotton wool or paint. Stick the clouds onto A3 paper adding the balloons so that they overlaps the clouds. Discuss the colours and patterns as you work. Help the children to add baskets cut from corrugated paper and draw ropes to attach the baskets to the balloons. Finally, let the children draw passengers and stick them into the baskets.

Cut out and mount the pictures on a display board covered with blue paper. Add a red border of wavy border roll or cut a strip of plain red paper to fit.

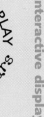

THEMES ON DISPLAY for early years

Add the title 'Up, up and away' cut from yellow paper letters and attach along the bottom of the display.

Make a model balloon from papier mâché to hang over the display by blowing up a balloon and covering it with three layers of newspaper, stuck down with watered-down PVA glue and a final layer of greaseproof paper.

Leave the balloon to dry in a warm place for two days, then burst the balloon with a pin. Paint the model and cut a circular hole into the base.

Thread a piece of string through the top of the model and attach a large button half way down to hold it in place. Tie a basket to the bottom and hang over the display.

Make mosaic balloons using squares of coloured paper stuck onto balloon outlines. Ask one of the children in each group to spread glue onto a section of the balloon and ask the rest of the group to find squares of a particular colour to stick down.

Talk about
● What might you see from a hot-air balloon?

● How else can we get high off the ground? (Climbing a tall building or flying in a plane.)
● Talk about other forms of flight.

Home links
● Give the children a balloon each to take home to remind them of the work that they have done.

Using the display
Language and literacy
● Read the story *Mrs Jolly's Brolly*, all about a jolly witch who joins in a hot-air balloon race.
● Fill paper balloon shapes with simple writing patterns for the children to write over in coloured pen.

Mathematical development
● Use the display to develop an understanding of 'high' and 'low' by asking individual children to point out the highest and lowest balloons.

Knowledge and understanding of the world
● Blow air into a balloon and let it out again. Ask the children what is making it change shape. Let them feel the air coming out of the balloon. Do not let children inflate balloons themselves.
● Tie up an air-filled balloon and pat it up towards the ceiling. Explain that the air inside is making it light and bouncy.

Physical development
● Use climbing apparatus to reinforce the children's understanding of 'high' and 'low'. Can they climb a bit higher? What can they see from the top of the slide?
● Work with the children, stretching up high and crouching down low. Try to reach an apple from the highest branch of an imaginary tree.

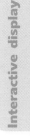

THEMES ON DISPLAY for early years

A ride on a steam train

Learning objectives: to use everyday words to describe position; to extend vocabulary, exploring the meanings and sounds of new words.

What you need
Powder paint in yellow, green, blue, brown, red and white; painting plates; sugar paper; scissors; pencil; rectangular painting sponge; paintbrushes; *The Train Ride* by Stephen Lambert (Walker Books); a toy train set; a whistle; toy cows; play people; model houses; toy trees and a station; books such as *Oi! Get off our Train* by John Burningham (Red Fox); *Thomas the Tank Engine* story-books by Reverend Awdry (Heinemann); factual books about trains; model trains made from shoeboxes; dolls; teddies.

What to do
Read *The Train Ride* to give the children the feel of what it would be like riding in a steam train through the countryside. Using a toy train and a whistle, encourage the children to join in with the sound effects as you tell the story. Set up a train track on the table with cows in the field, play people, model houses, trees and a station for one group of children to play with at a time.

Set out a painting table with plates of blue and white paint. Using A1 sheets of buff-coloured sugar paper, show a group of children how to dip their fingers into the paint and use their fingertips like brushes to paint a sky across the paper in wavy lines. Encourage them to cover the paper but not to lose the finger patterns by overworking it.

Set the 'sky' to one side to dry then pin it to the top half of the display board. Replace the blue and white paint with pots of yellow and greens. Draw hill shapes onto large sheets of sugar paper and ask the children to paint in each hill section in a different shade. Cut out the hills when the paint has dried and add them to the display board so that they overlap the sky.

A Train Ride

For the bottom section of the display, provide pots of blue, white and green paint and three large sheets of paper. Ask the children to paint the water and grass using large brushes.

Measure out the viaduct and draw it onto sugar paper to fit your display board. Once the outline has been drawn, show the children how to sponge-print bricks onto the paper using a rectangular sponge and brown paint. Draw lines to show the children where to print the bricks and work with one child at a time. Make sure that the viaduct is completely dry before cutting it out and adding it to the display.

Sketch out a train to fit the length of the viaduct and let individual children paint the engine, carriages, driver and passengers. Cut it out and stick it onto the centre of the viaduct.

Add a heading and a plain border in a contrasting colour such as purple or red, some toy trains for the display table along with books and a model train made out of shoeboxes to carry teddy bears and dolls.

Talk about
● Ask the children if they have been on a steam train. Talk about how the driver shovels coal in to make steam and compare this with modern trains.

● Using the toy train set, show the children why we need bridges and viaducts to cross water, valleys and roads. Have they heard of the Channel Tunnel that goes under the sea?
● Think about the people who work on the railways such as the driver, station master, guard, ticket collector, engineer and so on.
● Find some factual books about trains and talk about the different things that goods trains, mail trains and passenger trains carry.

Home links
● Ask the children to bring in a toy train for the display or a train book to be read at story-time.
● Ask some parents to help with a visit to your local station to watch the trains.

Using the display
Language and literacy
● Make name trains with the children's names spelled out as a puzzle, using one letter on each truck and the capital letter on the engine.
● Make a birthday train with a truck for each month of the year. Put the children's name cards in the trucks.

Mathematical development
● Introduce the words 'over' and 'under', 'up' and 'down', 'pull' and 'push', 'fast' and 'slow' as you tell stories and play alongside the children.
● Make a long train out of Duplo and count the trucks. Use for teaching 'one more' and 'one less'.

Physical development
● Move like trains, pulling heavy trucks slowly up a hill, then whizzing down the other side.
● Build bridges and tunnels for the toy trains.

At the airport

Learning objectives: to work as a group, taking turns and sharing fairly.

What you need
A toy plane; play people; small airport vehicles; cardboard boxes; a large shoebox; coloured card; coloured craft paper; a paper plate; a box lid; gold and silver paint; paintbrushes; black paper; labels; pens; scissors; books such as *Flight* by Kim Taylor in the *Flying Start* series (Belitha Press).

What to do
Cover a display table with black paper then cut simple skyscraper shapes from the sides of a cardboard box. Ask a group of children to paint them with gold and silver paint, and arrange them at the back of the display. Now cover two cardboard boxes with purple craft paper. Add doors, windows and signs for 'passenger lounge', 'in', 'out' and so on to the boxes to turn them into airport buildings.

Stick a paper plate onto the centre of a box lid and write a large 'H' in the centre to make a helicopter pad. Use a piece of coloured card for the runway and arrange a toy aeroplane and other vehicles on the display so that they can be used to carry the cases, the food and the fuel. Add some play people, a paper flag and a label saying 'Airport'.

Let the children play with the 'airport' in small groups, emphasizing the importance of playing together, taking turns and sharing fairly.

Encourage the children to think about where the people are going and why, and extend their vocabulary by talking to them as they play.

Set up the home corner as a travel agent's with brochures and posters. Ask the children to think about where they would like to go, how they will get there and what they would like to do there.

Talk about
● Have the children ever been on a flight? Introduce words such as 'luggage', 'tickets', 'arrive' and 'depart'.
● Talk about different forms of air travel (helicopter, plane, hot-air balloon).

Home links
● Ask parents if their children could bring in photos taken on holidays abroad or postcards sent from friends in other countries. Find out where the pictures were taken and introduce the names of other countries.

Other display table ideas
● Set up a table as a railway station, in the same way. Set out the train track and provide trains, play people and other props for the children to play with. Add signs for the station name and 'waiting room'.

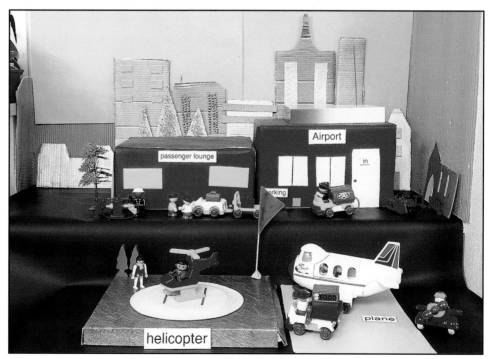

Can I help you?

Firefighter

Police officer

Refuse worker

Crossing patrol person

Doctor

Postal worker

Weather shapes

Pet shop dog

Leaf designs

Owl and squirrel

Run, rabbit, run

The mole and the hedgehog

The gingerbread house

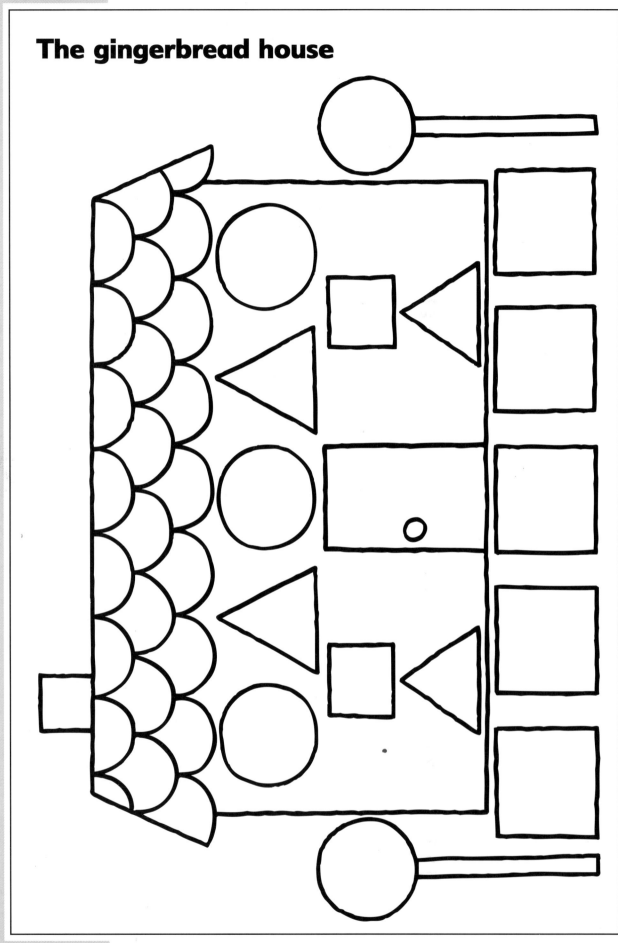

OUR WORLD